CAPITALISM

AND THE

HISTORIANS

CAPITALISM

AND THE

HISTORIANS

Edited with an Introduction by

F. A. HAYEK

Essays by

T. S. ASHTON

L. M. HACKER

W. H. HUTT

B. DE JOUVENEL

Phoenix Books

THE UNIVERSITY OF CHICAGO PRESS

THE UNIVERSITY OF CHICAGO PRESS, CHICAGO & LONDON
The University of Toronto Press, Toronto 5, Canada

Preface

The first three papers in this volume were originally presented to a gathering of an international group of economists, historians, and social philosophers who for some years have been meeting regularly to discuss the problems of the preservation of a free society against the totalitarian threat. One of the topics of discussion at the meeting of this Mont Pélèrin Society held at Beauvallon in France in September, 1951, was the treatment of capitalism by the historians. Of the four papers which served as the basis for the discussion, one, by Professor M. Silberschmidt of Zürich, is unfortunately not available in writing; nor is there a transcript of the lively discussion which ensued. It was felt by the participants in the discussion that the three written papers ought to be published, and it was suggested that this might be usefully combined with reprinting some earlier papers by members of the Society dealing with closely connected topics. Charged with the execution of this plan, I have tried, in an Introduction which draws heavily on what I have learned in the discussion, to explain the wider significance of the problem discussed in the following pages.

Preface

The second paper by Professor Ashton contained in the volume originally appeared in the *Journal of Economic History*, Supplement IX, 1949, and the paper by Professor Hutt in *Economica* for March, 1926. I have to thank the editors and publishers of both journals for the permission to reprint these articles.

F. A. Hayek

Contents

INTRODUCTION

INTRODUCTION

History and Politics

F. A. HAYEK

Political opinion and views about historical events ever have been and always must be closely connected. Past experience is the foundation on which our beliefs about the desirability of different policies and institutions are mainly based, and our present political views inevitably affect and color our interpretation of the past. Yet, if it is too pessimistic a view that man learns nothing from history, it may well be questioned whether he always learns the truth. While the events of the past are the source of the experience of the human race, their opinions are determined not by the objective facts but by the records and interpretations to which they have access. Few men will deny that our views about the goodness or badness of different institutions are largely determined by what we believe to have been their effects in the past. There is scarcely a political ideal or concept which does not involve opinions about a whole series of past events, and there are few historical memories which do not serve as a symbol of some political aim. Yet the historical beliefs which guide us in the present are not always in accord with the facts; sometimes they are even the effects rather than the cause of political beliefs. Historical myths have perhaps played nearly as great a role in shaping opinion as historical facts. Yet we can hardly hope to profit from past experience unless the facts from which we draw our conclusions are correct.

The influence which the writers of history thus exercise on public opinion is probably more immediate and extensive than that of the political theorists who launch new ideas. It seems as though even such new ideas reach wider circles usually not in their abstract form but as the interpretations of particular events. The historian is in this respect at least one step nearer to direct power over public opinion than is the theorist. And long before the professional historian takes up his pen, current controversy about recent events will have created a definite picture, or perhaps several different pictures, of these events which will affect contemporary discussion as much as any division on the merits of new issues.

This profound influence which current views about history have on political opinion is today perhaps less understood than it was in the past. One reason for this probably is the pretension of many modern historians to be purely scientific and completely free from all political prejudice. There can be no question, of course, that this is an imperative duty of the scholar in so far as historical research, that is, the ascertainment of the facts, is concerned. There is indeed no legitimate reason why, in answering questions of fact, historians of different political opinions should not be able to agree. But at the very beginning, in deciding which questions are worth asking, individual value judgments are bound to come in. And it is more than doubtful whether a connected history of a period or of a set of events could be written without interpreting these in the light, not only of theories about the interconnection of social processes, but also of definite values—or at least whether such a history would be worth reading. Historiography, as distinguished from historical research, is not only at least as much an art as a science; the writer who attempts it without being aware that his task is one of interpretation in the light of definite values also will succeed merely in deceiving himself and will become the victim of his unconscious prejudices.

There is perhaps no better illustration of the manner in which for more than a century the whole political ethos of a nation, and for a shorter time of most of the Western world, was shaped by the writings of a group of historians than the influence exercised by the English "Whig interpretation of history." It is probably no exaggeration to say that, for every person who had first-hand acquaintance with the writings of the political philosophers who founded the liberal tradition, there were fifty or a hundred who had absorbed it from the writings of men like Hallam and Macaulay or Grote and

Lord Acton. It is significant that the modern English historian who more than any other has endeavored to discredit this Whig tradition later came to write that "those who, perhaps in the misguided austerity of youth, wish to drive out that Whig interpretation . . . are sweeping a room which humanly speaking cannot long remain empty. They are opening the doors for seven devils which, precisely because they are newcomers, are bound to be worse than this first."[1] And, although he still suggests that "Whig history" was "wrong" history, he emphasizes that it "was one of our assets" and that "it had a wonderful effect on English politics."[2]

Whether in any relevant sense "Whig history" really was wrong history is a matter on which the last word has probably not yet been said but which we cannot discuss here. Its beneficial effect in creating the essentially liberal atmosphere of the nineteenth century is beyond doubt and was certainly not due to any misrepresentation of facts. It was mainly political history, and the chief facts on which it was based were known beyond question. It may not stand up in all respects to modern standards of historical research, but it certainly gave the generations brought up on it a true sense of the value of the political liberty which their ancestors had achieved

1. Herbert Butterfield, *The Englishman and His History* (Cambridge: Cambridge University Press, 1944), p. 3.

2. *Ibid.*, p. 7.

for them, and it served them as a guide in preserving that achievement.

The Whig interpretation of history has gone out of fashion with the decline of liberalism. But it is more than doubtful whether, because history now claims to be more scientific, it has become a more reliable or trustworthy guide in those fields where it has exercised most influence on political views. Political history indeed has lost much of the power and fascination it had in the nineteenth century; and it is doubtful whether any historical work of our time has had a circulation or direct influence comparable with, say, Macaulay's *History of England.* Yet the extent to which our present political views are colored by historical beliefs has certainly not diminished. As interest has shifted from the constitutional to the social and economic field, so the historical beliefs which act as driving forces are now mainly beliefs about economic history. It is probably justifiable to speak of a socialist interpretation of history which has governed political thinking for the last two or three generations and which consists mainly of a particular view of economic history. The remarkable thing about this view is that most of the assertions to which it has given the status of "facts which everybody knows" have long been proved not to have been facts at all; yet they still continue, outside the circle of professional economic historians, to be almost universally accepted as the basis for the estimate of the existing economic order.

Most people, when being told that their political convictions have been affected by particular views on economic history, will answer that they never have been interested in it and never have read a book on the subject. This, however, does not mean that they do not, with the rest, regard as established facts many of the legends which at one time or another have been given currency by writers on economic history. Although in the indirect and circuitous process by which new political ideas reach the general public the historian holds a key position, even he operates chiefly through many further relays. It is only at several removes that the picture which he provides becomes general property; it is via the novel and the newspaper, the cinema and political speeches, and ultimately the school and common talk that the ordinary person acquires his conceptions of history. But in the end even those who never read a book and probably have never heard the names of the historians whose views have influenced them come to see the past through their spectacles. Certain beliefs, for instance, about the evolution and effects of trade-unions, the alleged progressive growth of monopoly, the deliberate destruction of commodity stock as the result of competition (an event which, in fact, whenever it happened, was always the result of monopoly and usually of government-organized monopoly), about the suppression of beneficial inventions, the causes and effects of "imperialism," and the role of the armament industries or of "capitalists" in general in causing war, have become part of the folklore of our time. Most people would be greatly surprised to learn that most of what they believe about these subjects are not safely established facts but myths, launched from political motifs and then spread by people of good will into whose general beliefs they fitted. It would require several books like the present one to show how most of what is commonly believed on these questions, not merely by radicals but also by many conservatives, is not history but political legend. All we can do here with regard to these topics is to refer the reader to a few works from which he can inform himself about the present state of knowledge on the more important of them.[3]

There is, however, one supreme myth which more than any other has served to discredit the economic sys-

3. Cf. M. Dorothy George, "The Combination Laws Reconsidered," *Economic History* (supplement to the *Economic Journal*), I (May, 1927), 214–28; W. H. Hutt, *The Theory of Collective Bargaining* (London: P. S. King & Son, 1930) and *The Economists and the Public* (London: J. Cape, 1936); L. C. Robbins, *The Economic Basis of Class Conflict* (London: Macmillan & Co., 1939) and *The Economic Causes of War* (London: J. Cape, 1939); Walter Sulzbach, *"Capitalistic Warmongers": A Modern Superstition* ("Public Policy Pamphlets," No. 35 [Chicago: University of Chicago Press, 1942]); G. J. Stigler, "Competition in the United States," in *Five Lectures on Economic Problems* (London and New York: Longmans, Green & Co., 1949); G. Warren Nutter, *The Extent of Enterprise Monopoly in the United States, 1899–1939* (Chicago: University of Chicago Press, 1951); and, on most of these problems, the writings of Ludwig von Mises, especially his *Socialism* (London: J. Cape, 1936).

tem to which we owe our present-day civilization and to the examination of which the present volume is devoted. It is the legend of the deterioration of the position of the working classes in consequence of the rise of "capitalism" (or of the "manufacturing" or the "industrial system"). Who has not heard of the "horrors of early capitalism" and gained the impression that the advent of this system brought untold new suffering to large classes who before were tolerably content and comfortable? We might justly hold in disrepute a system to which the blame attached that even for a time it worsened the position of the poorest and most numerous class of the population. The widespread emotional aversion to "capitalism" is closely connected with this belief that the undeniable growth of wealth which the competitive order has produced was purchased at the price of depressing the standard of life of the weakest elements of society.

That this was the case was at one time indeed widely taught by economic historians. A more careful examination of the facts has, however, led to a thorough refutation of this belief. Yet, a generation after the controversy has been decided, popular opinion still continues as though the older belief had been true. How this belief should ever have arisen and why it should continue to determine the general view long after it has been disproved are both problems which deserve serious examination.

This kind of opinion can be frequently found not only in the political literature hostile to capitalism but even in works which on the whole are sympathetic to the political tradition of the nineteenth century. It is well represented by the following passage from Ruggiero's justly esteemed *History of European Liberalism:*

Thus it was precisely at the period of intensest industrial growth that the condition of the labourer changed for the worse. Hours of labour multiplied out of all measure; the employment of women and children in factories lowered wages: the keen competition between the workers themselves, no longer tied to their parishes but free to travel and congregate where they were most in demand, further cheapened the labour they placed on the market: numerous and frequent industrial crises, inevitable at a period of growth, when population and consumption are not yet stabilized, swelled from time to time the ranks of the unemployed, the reserves in the army of starvation.[4]

There was little excuse for such a statement even when it appeared a quarter-century ago. A year after it was first published, the most eminent student of modern economic history, Sir John Clapham, rightly complained:

The legend that everything was getting worse for the working man, down to some unspecified date between the drafting of the People's Charter and the Great Exhibition, dies hard. The fact that, after the price fall of 1820-1, the purchasing power

4. Guido de Ruggiero, *Storia del liberalismo europeo* (Bari, 1925), trans. R. G. Collingwood (London: Oxford University Press, 1927), p. 47, esp. p. 85. It is interesting that Ruggiero seems to derive his facts mainly from another supposedly liberal historian, Élie Halévy, although Halévy never expressed them so crudely.

of wages in general—not, of course, of everyone's wages—was definitely greater than it had been just before the revolutionary and Napoleonic wars, fits so ill with the tradition that it is very seldom mentioned, the works of statisticians of wages and prices being constantly disregarded by social historians.[5]

In so far as general public opinion is concerned, the position is scarcely better today, although the facts have had to be conceded even by most of those who had been mainly responsible for spreading the contrary opinion. Few authors have done more to create the belief that the early nineteenth century had been a time in which the position of the working class had become particularly bad than Mr. and Mrs. J. L. Hammond; their books are frequently quoted to illustrate this. But toward the end of their lives they admitted candidly that

statisticians tell us that when they have put in order such data as they can find, they are satisfied that earnings increased and that most men and women were less poor when this discontent was loud and active than they were when the eighteenth century was beginning to grow old in a silence like that of autumn. The evidence, of course, is scanty, and its interpretation not too simple, but this general view is probably more or less correct.[6]

This did little to change the general effect their writing had had on public opinion. In one of the latest competent studies of the history of the Western political tradition,

5. J. H. Clapham, *An Economic History of Modern Britain* (Cambridge, 1926), I, 7.

6. J. L. and Barbara Hammond, *The Bleak Age* (1934) (rev. ed., London: Pelican Books, 1947), p. 15.

for instance, we can still read that, "like all the great social experiments, however, the invention of the labour market was expensive. It involved, in the first instance, a swift and drastic decline in the material standard of living of the working classes."[7]

I was going to continue here that this is still the view which is almost exclusively represented in the popular literature when the latest book by Bertrand Russell came to my hands in which, as if to confirm this, he blandly asserts:

The industrial revolution caused unspeakable misery both in England and in America. I do not think any student of economic history can doubt that the average happiness in England in the early nineteenth century was lower than it had been a hundred years earlier; and this was due almost entirely to scientific technique.[8]

The intelligent layman can hardly be blamed if he believes that such a categorical statement from a writer of this rank must be true. If a Bertrand Russell believes this, we must not be surprised that the versions of economic history which today are spread in hundreds of thousands of volumes of pocket editions are mostly of the kind which spread this old myth. It is also still a rare exception when we meet a work of historical fiction which dispenses with the dramatic touch which the story

7. Frederick Watkins, *The Political Tradition of the West* (Cambridge, Mass.: Harvard University Press, 1948), p. 213.

8. Bertrand Russell, *The Impact of Science on Society* (New York: Columbia University Press, 1951), pp. 19–20.

of the sudden worsening of the position of large groups of workers provides.

The true fact of the slow and irregular progress of the working class which we now know to have taken place is of course rather unsensational and uninteresting to the layman. It is no more than he has learned to expect as the normal state of affairs; and it hardly occurs to him that this is by no means an inevitable progress, that it was preceded by centuries of virtual stagnation of the position of the poorest, and that we have come to expect continuous improvement only as a result of the experience of several generations with the system which he still thinks to be the cause of the misery of the poor.

Discussions of the effects of the rise of modern industry on the working classes refer almost always to the conditions in England in the first half of the nineteenth century; yet the great change to which they refer had commenced much earlier and by then had quite a long history and had spread far beyond England. The freedom of economic activity which in England had proved so favorable to the rapid growth of wealth was probably in the first instance an almost accidental by-product of the limitations which the revolution of the seventeenth century had placed on the powers of government; and only after its beneficial effects had come to be widely noticed did the economists later undertake to explain the connection and to argue for the removal of the remaining barriers to commercial freedom. In many ways it is misleading to speak of "capitalism" as though this had been a new and altogether different system which suddenly came into being toward the end of the eighteenth century; we use this term here be- cause it is the most familiar name, but only with great reluctance, since with its modern connotations it is it- self largely a creation of that socialist interpretation of economic history with which we are concerned. The term is especially misleading when, as is often the case, it is connected with the idea of the rise of the propertyless proletariat, which by some devious process have been deprived of their rightful ownership of the tools for their work.

The actual history of the connection between capital- ism and the rise of the proletariat is almost the opposite of that which these theories of the expropriation of the masses suggest. The truth is that, for the greater part of history, for most men the possession of the tools for their work was an essential condition for survival or at least for being able to rear a family. The number of those who could maintain themselves by working for others, although they did not themselves possess the necessary equipment, was limited to a small proportion of the population. The amount of arable land and of tools handed down from one generation to the next limited the total number who could survive. To be left without them meant in most instances death by starva- tion or at least the impossibility of procreation. There

was little incentive and little possibility for one generation to accumulate the additional tools which would
have made possible the survival of a larger number of
the next, so long as the advantage of employing additional hands was limited mainly to the instances where
the division of the tasks increased the efficiency of the
work of the owner of the tools. It was only when the
larger gains from the employment of machinery provided both the means and the opportunity for their investment that what in the past had been a recurring surplus of population doomed to early death was in an
increasing measure given the possibility of survival.
Numbers which had been practically stationary for
many centuries began to increase rapidly. The proletariat
which capitalism can be said to have "created" was thus
not a proportion of the population which would have
existed without it and which it had degraded to a lower
level; it was an additional population which was enabled
to grow up by the new opportunities for employment
which capitalism provided. In so far as it is true that the
growth of capital made the appearance of the proletariat
possible, it was in the sense that it raised the productivity of labor so that much larger numbers of those
who had not been equipped by their parents with the necessary tools were enabled to maintain themselves by their
labor alone; but the capital had to be supplied first
before those were enabled to survive who afterward
claimed as a right a share in its ownership. Although

it was certainly not from charitable motives, it still was the first time in history that one group of people found it in their interest to use their earnings on a large scale to provide new instruments of production to be operated by those who without them could not have produced their own sustenance.

Of the effect of the rise of modern industry on the growth of population, statistics tell a vivid tale. That this in itself largely contradicts the common belief about the harmful effect of the rise of the factory system on the large masses is not the point with which we are at present concerned. Nor need we more than mention the fact that, so long as this increase of the numbers of those whose output reached a certain level brought forward a fully corresponding increase in population, the level of the poorest fringe could not be substantially improved, however much the average might rise. The point of immediate relevance is that this increase of population and particularly of the manufacturing population had proceeded in England at least for two or three generations before the period of which it is alleged that the position of the workers seriously deteriorated.

The period to which this refers is also the period when the problem of the position of the working class became for the first time one of general concern. And the opinions of some of the contemporaries are indeed the main sources of the present beliefs. Our first question must therefore be how it came about that such an impression contrary to the facts should have become widely held among the people then living.

One of the chief reasons was evidently an increasing awareness of facts which before had passed unnoticed. The very increase of wealth and well-being which had been achieved raised standards and aspirations. What for ages had seemed a natural and inevitable situation, or even as an improvement upon the past, came to be regarded as incongruous with the opportunities which the new age appeared to offer. Economic suffering both became more conspicuous and seemed less justified, because general wealth was increasing faster than ever before. But this, of course, does not prove that the people whose fate was beginning to cause indignation and alarm were worse off than their parents or grandparents had been. While there is every evidence that great misery existed, there is none that it was greater than or even as great as it had been before. The aggregations of large numbers of cheap houses of industrial workers were probably more ugly than the picturesque cottages in which some of the agricultural laborers or domestic workers had lived; and they were certainly more alarming to the landowner or to the city patrician than the poor dispersed over the country had been. But for those who had moved from country to town it meant an improvement; and even though the rapid growth of the industrial centers created sanitary problems with which people had yet slowly and painfully to learn to cope, statistics leave little doubt that even general health was on the whole benefited rather than harmed.[9]

More important, however, for the explanation of the change from an optimistic to a pessimistic view of the effects of industrialization than this awakening of social conscience was probably the fact that this change of opinion appears to have commenced, not in the manufacturing districts which had firsthand knowledge of what was happening, but in the political discussion of the English metropolis which was somewhat remote from, and had little part in, the new development. It is evident that the belief about the "horrible" conditions prevailing among the manufacturing populations of the Midlands and the north of England was in the 1830's and 1840's widely held among the upper classes of London and the south. It was one of the main arguments with which the landowning class hit back at the manufacturers to counter the agitation of the latter against the Corn Laws and for free trade. And it was from these arguments of the conservative press that the radical intelligentsia of the time, with little firsthand knowledge of the industrial districts, derived their views which were to become the standard weapons of political propaganda.

This position, to which so much even of the present-day beliefs about the effects of the rise of industrialism on the working classes can be traced, is well illustrated

9. Cf. M. C. Buer, *Health, Wealth and Population in the Early Days of the Industrial Revolution* (London: G. Routledge & Sons, 1926).

by a letter written about 1843 by a London lady, Mrs. Cooke Taylor, after she had for the first time visited some industrial districts of Lancashire. Her account of the conditions she found is prefaced by some remarks about the general state of opinion in London:

I need not remind you of the statements put forward in the newspapers, relative to the miserable conditions of the opera-tives, and the tyranny of their masters, for they made such an impression on me that it was with reluctance that I consented to go to Lancashire; indeed these misrepresentations are quite general, and people believe them without knowing why or wherefore. As an instance: just before starting I was at a large dinner party, at the west end of the town, and seated next a gentleman who is considered a very clever and intelligent man. In the course of the conversation I mentioned that I was going to Lancashire. He stared and asked," "What on earth could take me there? That he would as soon think of going to St. Giles's; that it was a horrid place—factories all over; that the people, from starvation, oppression, and over-work, had almost lost the form of humanity; and that the mill-owners were a bloated, pampered race, feeding on the very vitals of the people." I answered that this was a dreadful state of things; and asked "In what part he had seen such misery?" He replied, that "he had never *seen* it, but had been *told* that it existed; and that for his part he never *had been* in the manufacturing districts, and that he *never would*." This gentleman was one of the very numerous body of people who spread reports without ever tak-ing the trouble of inquiring if they be true or false.[10]

10. This letter is quoted in "Reuben," *A Brief History of the Rise and Progress of the Anti-Corn-Law League* (London, [1845]). Mrs. Cooke Taylor, who appears to have been the wife of the radical Dr. Cooke Taylor, had visited the factory of Henry Ashworth at Turton, near Bolton, then still a rural district and therefore probably more attractive than some of the urban industrial districts.

Mrs. Cooke Taylor's detailed description of the satisfactory state of affairs which to her surprise she found ends with the remark: "Now that I have seen the factory people at their work, in their cottages and in their schools, I am totally at a loss to account for the outcry that has been made against them. They are better clothed, better fed, and better conducted than many other classes of working people."[11]

But even if at the time itself the opinion which was later taken over by the historians was loudly voiced by one party, it remains to explain why the view of one party among the contemporaries, and that not of the radicals or liberals but of the Tories, should have become the almost uncontradicted view of the economic historians of the second half of the century. The reason for this seems to have been that the new interest in economic history was itself closely associated with the interest in socialism and that at first a large proportion of those who devoted themselves to the study of economic history were inclined toward socialism. It was not merely the great stimulus which Karl Marx's "materialist interpretation of history" undoubtedly gave to the study of economic history; practically all the socialist schools held a philosophy of history intended to show the relative character of the different economic institutions and the necessity of different economic systems succeeding each other in time. They all tried to prove that the

11. *Ibid.*

system which they attacked, the system of private property in the means of production, was a perversion of an earlier and more natural system of communal property; and, because the theoretical preconceptions which guided them postulated that the rise of capitalism must have been detrimental to the working classes, it is not surprising that they found what they were looking for.

But not only those by whom the study of economic history was consciously made a tool of political agitation—as is true in many instances from Marx and Engels to Werner Sombart and Sidney and Beatrice Webb—but also many of the scholars who sincerely believed that they were approaching the facts without prejudice produced results which were scarcely less biased. This was in part due to the fact that the "historical approach" which they adopted had itself been proclaimed as a counterblast to the theoretical analysis of classical economics, because the latter's verdict on the popular remedies for current complaints had so frequently been unfavorable.[12] It is no accident that the largest and most influential group of students of economic history in the sixty years preceding the first World

12. Merely as an illustration of the general attitude of that school a characteristic statement of one of its best-known representatives, Adolf Held, may be quoted. According to him, it was David Ricardo "in whose hand orthodox economics became the docile servant of the exclusive interests of mobile capital," and his theory of rent "was simply dictated by the hatred of the moneyed capitalist against the landowners" (*Zwei Bücher zur sozialen Geschichte Englands* [Leipzig: Duncker & Humblot, 1881], p. 178).

War, the German Historical School, prided themselves also in the name of the "socialist of the chair" (*Kathedersozialisten*); or that their spiritual successors, the American "institutionalists," were mostly socialists in their inclination. The whole atmosphere of these schools was such that it would have required an exceptional independence of mind for a young scholar not to succumb to the pressure of academic opinion. No reproach was more feared or more fatal to academic prospects than that of being an "apologist" of the capitalist system; and, even if a scholar dared to contradict dominant opinion on a particular point, he would be careful to safeguard himself against such accusation by joining in the general condemnation of the capitalist system.[13] To treat the existing economic order as merely a "historical phase" and to be able to predict from the "laws of historical development" the emergence of a better future system became the hallmark of what was then regarded as the truly scientific spirit.

Much of the misrepresentation of the facts by the earlier economic historians was, in reality, directly traceable to a genuine endeavor to look at these facts without any theoretical preconceptions. The idea that one can trace the causal connections of any events without

13. A good account of the general political atmosphere prevailing among the German Historical School of economists will be found in Ludwig Pohle, *Die gegenwärtige Krise in der deutschen Volkswirtschaftslehre* (Leipzig, 1911).

employing a theory, or that such a theory will emerge automatically from the accumulation of a sufficient amount of facts, is of course sheer illusion. The complexity of social events in particular is such that, without the tools of analysis which a systematic theory provides, one is almost bound to misinterpret them; and those who eschew the conscious use of an explicit and tested logical argument usually merely become the victims of the popular beliefs of their time. Common sense is a treacherous guide in this field, and what seem "obvious" explanations frequently are no more than commonly accepted superstitions. It may seem obvious that the introduction of machinery will produce a general reduction of the demand for labor. But persistent effort to think the problem through shows that this belief is the result of a logical fallacy, of stressing one effect of the assumed change and leaving out others. Nor do the facts give any support to the belief. Yet anyone who thinks it to be true is very likely to find what seems to him confirming evidence. It is easy enough to find in the early nineteenth century instances of extreme poverty and to draw the conclusion that this must have been the effect of the introduction of machinery, without asking whether conditions had been any better or perhaps even worse before. Or one may believe that an increase of production must lead to the impossibility of selling all the product and, when one then finds a stagnation of sales, regard this as a confirmation of the expectations, although there are several more plausible explanations than general "overproduction" or "underconsumption."

There can be no doubt that many of these misrepresentations were put forward in good faith; and there is no reason why we should not respect the motives of some of those who, to arouse public conscience, painted the misery of the poor in the blackest colors. We owe to agitation of this kind, which forced unwilling eyes to face unpleasant facts, some of the finest and most generous acts of public policy—from the abolition of slavery to the removal of taxes on imported food and the destruction of many intrenched monopolies and abuses. And there is every reason to remember how miserable the majority of the people still were as recently as a hundred or a hundred and fifty years ago. But we must not, long after the event, allow a distortion of the facts, even if committed out of humanitarian zeal, to affect our view of what we owe to a system which for the first time in history made people feel that this misery might be avoidable. The very claims and ambitions of the working classes were and are the result of the enormous improvement of their position which capitalism brought about. There were, no doubt, many people whose privileged position, whose power to secure a comfortable income by preventing others from doing better what they were being paid for, was destroyed by the advance of freedom of enterprise. There may be various other grounds on which the development of modern industrialism might be deplored by some; certain aesthetic and moral values to which the privileged upper classes attached great importance were no doubt endangered by it. Some people might even question whether the rapid increase of population, or, in other words, the decrease in infant mortality, was a blessing. But if, and in so far as, one takes as one's test the effect on the standard of life of the large number of the toiling classes, there can be little doubt that this effect was to produce a general upward trend.

The recognition of this fact by the students had to wait for the rise of a generation of economic historians who no longer regarded themselves as the opponents of economics, intent upon proving that the economists had been wrong, but who were themselves trained economists who devoted themselves to the study of economic evolution. Yet the results which this modern economic history had largely established a generation ago have still gained little recognition outside professional circles. The process by which the results of research ultimately become general property has in this instance proved to be even slower than usual.[14] The new results in this case have not been of the kind which is avidly picked up by the intellectuals because it readily fits into their general prejudices but, on the contrary, are of a kind which is in conflict with their general beliefs. Yet, if we

14. On this cf. my essay, "The Intellectuals and Socialism," *University of Chicago Law Review*, Vol. XVI (1949).

have been right in our estimate of the importance which erroneous views have had in shaping political opinion, it is high time that the truth at last displace the legend which has so long governed popular belief. It was the conviction that this revision was long overdue which led to this topic being put on the program of the meeting at which the first three of the following papers were originally presented and then to the decision that they should be made available to a wider public.

The recognition that the working class as a whole benefited from the rise of modern industry is of course entirely compatible with the fact that some individuals or groups in this as well as other classes may for a time have suffered from its results. The new order meant an increased rapidity of change, and the quick increase of wealth was largely the result of the increased speed of adaptation to change which made it possible. In those spheres where the mobility of a highly competitive market became effective, the increased range of opportunities more than compensated for the greater instability of particular jobs. But the spreading of the new order was gradual and uneven. There remained—and there remains to the present day—pockets which, while fully exposed to the vicissitudes of the markets for their products, are too isolated to benefit much from the opportunities which the market opened elsewhere. The various instances of the decline of old crafts which were displaced by a mechanical process have been widely publicized (the fate of the hand-loom weavers is the classical example always quoted). But even there it is more than doubtful whether the amount of suffering caused is comparable to that which a series of bad harvests in any region would have caused before capitalism had greatly increased the mobility of goods and of capital. The incidence on a small group among a prospering community is probably felt more of an injustice and a challenge then was the general suffering of earlier times which was considered as unalterable fate.

The understanding of the true sources of the grievances, and still more the manner in which they might be remedied so far as possible, presupposes a better comprehension of the working of the market system than most of the earlier historians possessed. Much that has been blamed on the capitalist system is in fact due to remnants or revivals of precapitalistic features: to monopolistic elements which were either the direct result of ill-conceived state action or the consequence of a failure to understand that a smooth working competitive order required an appropriate legal framework. We have already referred to some of the features and tendencies for which capitalism is usually blamed and which are in fact due to its basic mechanism not being allowed to work; and the question, in particular, why and to what extent monopoly has interfered with its beneficial operation is too big a problem to attempt to say more about it here.

F. A. Hayek

This introduction is not intended to do more than to indicate the general setting in which the more specific discussion of the following papers must be seen. For its inevitable tendency to run in generalities I trust these special studies will make up by the very concrete treatment of their particular problems. They cover merely part of the wider issue, since they were intended to provide the factual basis for the discussion which they opened. Of the three related questions—What were the facts? How did the historians present them?and Why?—they deal primarily with the first and chiefly by implication with the second. Only the paper by M. de Jouvenel, which therefore possesses a somewhat different character, addresses itself mainly to the third question; and, in so doing, it raises problems which reach even beyond the complex of questions which have been sketched here.

PART I

1

The Treatment of Capitalism
by Historians

T. S. ASHTON

To occupy a chair of economic history in the University
of London means that, instead of being able to give
one's vacation to the refreshment of body and spirit or
the pursuit of knowledge, one is forced to spend much
of it in reading examination scripts produced not only
by one's own students but also by several hundred young
men and women in all parts of Britain and, indeed, in
the uttermost parts of the earth. This situation is un-
enviable. But at least it enables one to speak with
assurance about the ideas held about the economic past
by those who, in a short time, will be holding positions
of authority in industry, commerce, journalism, politics,
and administration and will therefore be influential in
forming what we call "public opinion."

It is a truism that men's political and economic ideas
depend as much on the experiences of the preceding
generation as on the needs of their own. Asked by Lionel
Robbins what they considered to be the outstanding
problem of today, the majority of a class of students at

the School of Economics answered unhesitatingly, "To maintain full employment." After a decade of full, or overfull, employment in England, the shadow of the 1930's hides from large numbers the real problems of postwar England. There is, however, a deeper shadow that obscures reality and darkens counsels. It is cast by the grievances—real or alleged—of workingmen who lived and died a century ago. According to a large number of the scripts which it has been my lot to read, the course of English history since about the year 1760 to the setting-up of the welfare state in 1945 was marked by little but toil and sweat and oppression. Economic forces, it would appear, are by nature malevolent. Every labor-saving device has led to a decline of skill and to an increase of unemployment. Is it not well known that, when prices rise, wages lag behind, and the standard of life of the workers falls? But what if prices fall? Is it not equally well known that this must result in a depression of trade and industry, a fall of wages and unemployment, so that, once more, the standard of life of the workers falls?

Modern youth is prone to melancholy; like Rachel, it refuses to be comforted. Yet I think it is something more than adolescent pessimism that is responsible for this climate of opinion. Students attend lectures and read textbooks, and it is a matter of common prudence to pay some heed to what they have heard and read. A good deal—indeed, far too much—of what appears in the scripts is literal reproduction of the spoken or written word. Much the greater part of the responsibility must lie with the professional economic historian.

The student of English economic history is fortunate in having at his disposal the reports of a long series of Royal Commissions and Committees of Inquiry beginning in the eighteenth century but reaching full stream in the 1830's, 1840's, and 1850's. These reports are one of the glories of the early Victorian age. They signalized a quickening of social conscience, a sensitiveness to distress, that had not been evident in any other period or in any other country. Scores of massive folios provided statistical and verbal evidence that all was not well with large numbers of the people of England and called the attention of legislators and the reading public to the need for reform. The economic historians of the succeeding generations could do no other than draw on their findings; and scholarship, no less than society, benefited. There was, however, loss as well as gain. A picture of the economic system constructed from Blue Books dealing with social grievances, and not with the normal processes of economic development, was bound to be one-sided. It is such a picture of early Victorian society that has become fixed in the minds of popular writers and is reproduced in my scripts. A careful reading of the reports would, indeed, lead to the conclusion that much that was wrong was the result of laws, customs, habits, and forms of organization that belonged to earlier periods and were rapidly becoming obsolete. It would have brought home to the mind that it was not among the factory employees but among the domestic workers, whose traditions and methods were those of the eighteenth century, that earnings were at their lowest. It would have provided evidence that it was not in the large establishments making use of steam power but in the garret or cellar workshops that conditions of employment were at their worst. It would have led to the conclusion that it was not in the growing manufacturing towns or the developing coal fields but in remote villages and the countryside that restrictions on personal freedom and the evils of truck were most marked. But few had the patience to go carefully through these massive volumes. It was so much easier to pick out the more sensational evidences of distress and work them into a dramatic story of exploitation. The result has been that a generation that had the enterprise and industry to assemble the facts, the honesty to reveal them, and the energy to set about the task of reform has been held up to obloquy as the author, not of the Blue Books, but of the evils themselves. Conditions in the mills and the factory town were so bad, it seemed, that there must have been deterioration; and, since the supposed deterioration had taken place at a time when machinery had increased, the machines, and those who owned them, must have been responsible.

At the same time the romantic revival in literature

led to an idyllic view of the life of the present. The idea that agriculture is the only natural and healthy activity for human beings has persisted, and indeed spread, as more of us have escaped from the curse of Adam—or, as the tedious phrase goes, "become divorced from the soil." A year ago an examinee remarked profoundly that "in earlier centuries agriculture was widespread in England" but added sorrowfully, "Today it is confined to the rural areas." There was a similar idealization of the condition of the domestic worker, who had taken only the first step in the proceedings for divorce. Bear with me while I read some passages with which Friedrich Engels (who is usually acclaimed a realist) opens his account of *The Condition of the Working Classes in England in 1844.* It is, of course, based on the writings of the Reverend Philip Gaskell, whose earnestness and honesty are not in doubt, but whose mind had not been confused by any study of history. Engels' book opens with the declaration that "the history of the proletariat in England begins with the invention of the steam-engine and of machinery for working cotton." Before their time, he continues,

the workers vegetated throughout a passably comfortable exist-ence, leading a righteous and peaceful life in all piety and probity; and their material condition was far better than that of their successors. They did not need to overwork; they did no more than they chose to do, and yet earned what they needed. They had leisure for healthful work in garden or field, work which, in itself, was recreation for them, and they could take part beside in the recreation and games of their neighbours, and all these games—bowling, cricket, football, etc. contributed to their physical health and vigour. They were, for the most part, strong, well-built people, in whose physique little or no difference from that of their peasant neighbours was discoverable. Their children grew up in fresh country air, and, if they could help their parents at work, it was only occasionally; while of eight or twelve hours work for them there was no question.[1]

It is difficult to say whether this or the lurid picture of the lives of the grandchildren of these people presented in later pages of the book is more completely at variance with the facts. Engels had no doubt whatsoever as to the cause of the deterioration in the condition of labor. "The proletariat," he repeats, "was called into existence by the introduction of machinery." "The consequences of improvement in machinery under our present social conditions," he asserts, "are, for the working-man, solely injurious, and often in the highest degree oppressive. Every new advance brings with it loss of employment, want and suffering."

1. London, 1892. Engels continues: "They were 'respectable' people, good husbands and fathers, led moral lives because they had no temptation to be immoral, there being no groggeries or low houses in their vicinity, and because the host, at whose inn they now and then quenched their thirst, was also a respectable man, usually a large tenant farmer who took pride in his good order, good beer, and early hours. They had their children the whole day at home, and brought them up in obedience and the fear of God. . . . The young people grew up in idyllic simplicity and intimacy with their playmates until they married, etc."

Engels has had many disciples, even among those who do not accept the historical materialism of Marx, with which such views are generally connected. Hostility to the machine is associated with hostility to its products and, indeed, to all innovation in consumption. One of the outstanding accomplishments of the new industrial age is to be seen in the greatly increased supply and variety of fabrics offered on the market. Yet the changes in dress are taken as evidence of growing poverty: "The clothing of the working-people in a majority of cases," Engels declares, "is in a very bad condition. The material used for it is not of the best adapted. Wool and linen have almost vanished from the wardrobes of both sexes, and cotton has taken their place. Skirts are made of bleached or coloured cotton goods, and woollen petticoats are rarely to be seen on the wash-line." The truth is that they never had been greatly displayed on the wash line, for woolen goods are liable to shrink. The workers of earlier periods had to make their garments last (second or third hand as many of these were), and soap and water were inimical to the life of clothing. The new, cheap textiles may not have been as hard-wearing as broadcloth, but they were more abundant; and the fact that they could be washed without suffering harm had a bearing, if not on their own life, at least on the lives of those who wore them.

The same hostility is shown to innovation in food and drink. Generations of writers have followed William

Cobbett in his hatred of tea. One would have thought that the enormous increase in consumption between the beginning of the eighteenth and the middle of the nineteenth century was one element in a rising standard of comfort; but only a few years ago Professor Parkinson asserted that it was "growing poverty" that made tea increasingly essential to the lower classes as ale was put beyond their means."[2] (This, I may add, unfortunately meant that they were forced to consume sugar, and one must suppose that this practice also led to a fall in the standard of living.) Similarly, Dr. Salaman has recently assured us that the introduction of the potato into the diet of the workers at this time was a factor detrimental to health and that it enabled the employers to force down the level of wages—which, it is well known, is always determined by the minimum of food required for subsistence.[3]

Very gradually those who held to these pessimistic views of the effects of industrial change have been forced to yield ground. The painstaking researches of Bowley and Wood have shown that over most of this period, and later, the course of real wages was upward. The proof is not at all easy, for it is clear that there were sections of the working classes of whom it was emphat-

2. C. N. Parkinson, *Trade in the Eastern Seas* (Cambridge, 1937), p. 94.

3. R. N. Salaman, *The History and Social Influence of the Potato* (Cambridge, 1949).

ically not true. In the first half of the nineteenth century the population of England was growing, partly because of natural increase, partly as the result of the influx of Irish. For those endowed with little or no skill, marginal productivity, and hence earnings, remained low. A large part of their incomes was spent on commodities (mainly food, drink, and housing), the cost of which had hardly been affected by technical development. That is why so many of the economists, like McCulloch and Mill, were themselves dubious about the beneficial nature of the industrial system. There were, however, large and growing sections of skilled and better-paid workers whose money incomes were rising and who had a substantial margin to spend on the products of the machine, the costs of which were falling progressively. The controversy really rests on which of the groups was increasing most. Generally it is now agreed that for the majority the gain in real wages was substantial.

But this does not dispose of the controversy. Real earnings might have risen, it was said, but it was the quality of life and not the quantity of goods consumed that mattered. In particular, it was the evil conditions of housing and the insanitary conditions of the towns that were called as evidence that the circumstances of labor had worsened. "Everything which here arouses horror and indignation," wrote Engels of Manchester in 1844, "is of recent origin, belongs to the industrial epoch"— and the reader is left to infer that the equally repulsive features of cities like Dublin and Edinburgh, which were scarcely touched by the new industry, were, somehow or other, also the product of the machine.

This is the legend that has spread round the world and has determined the attitude of millions of men and women to labor-saving devices and to those who own them. Indians and Chinese, Egyptians and Negroes, to whose fellow-countrymen today the dwellings of the English of the mid-nineteenth century would be wealth indeed, solemnly declare, in the scripts I have to read, that the English workers were living in conditions unworthy of beasts. They write with indignation about the inefficiency of the sanitation and the absence of civic amenities—the very nature of which is still unknown to the urban workers of a large part of the earth.

Now, no one who has read the reports of the Committee on the Sanitary Condition of the Working Classes of 1842 or that of the Commission on the Health of Towns of 1844 can doubt that the state of affairs was, from the point of view of modern Western civilization, deplorable. But, equally, no one who has read Dorothy George's account of living conditions in London in the eighteenth century can be sure that they had deteriorated.[4] Dr. George herself believes that they had improved, and Clapham declared that the English towns of the

4. M. Dorothy George, *London Life in the Eighteenth Century* (London: K. Paul, Trench, Trubner; New York: A. A. Knopf, 1926).

mid-century were "less crowded than the great towns of other countries and not, universally, more insanitary."[5] The question I wish to raise, however, is that of responsibility. Engels, as we have seen, attributed the evils to the machine; others are no less emphatic in attributing them to the Industrial Revolution, which comes to much the same thing. No historian, as far as I know, has looked at the problem through the eyes of those who had the task of building and maintaining the towns.

There were two main aspects: the supply of houses in relation to the demand and the technical matters of drainage, sanitation, and ventilation. In the early nineteenth century, according to one of these scripts, "the workers were pressed into back-to-back houses, like sardines in a rabbit warren." Many of the houses were certainly unsubstantial and insanitary, and for this it is usual to blame the industrialist who put them up, a man commonly spoken of as the jerry-builder. I had often wondered who this man was. When I was young, the parson of the church I attended once preached a sermon on Jerry, who, he asserted with complete conviction, was at that very moment burning in hell for his crimes. I have searched for records of him, but in vain. It appears from Weekley's *Etymological Dictionary of Modern English* that "jerry" is a corruption of "jury"—a word of nautical origin applied to any part of a ship contrived for

5. J. H. Clapham, *An Economic History of Modern Britain* (Cambridge, 1926), I, 548.

temporary use, as in "jury mast" and "jury rig," and extended to other things, such as "jury leg" for "wooden leg." "Jerry," then, means temporary, or inferior, or makeshift; and no doubt other uses of the word as a makeshift in an emergency will come to the mind. According to Partridge's *Dictionary of Slang and Unconventional English,* it was first used in Liverpool about 1830. The place and time are significant. Liverpool was the port for the rapidly developing industrial area of southeastern Lancashire; it was the chief gate of entry for the swarms of Irish immigrants. It was probably here that the pressure of population on the supplies of accommodation was most acute. Houses were run up rapidly, and many of them were flimsy structures, the outer walls of which were only 4½ inches in thickness. On December 5, 1822, some of them, along with many buildings elsewhere, were blown down in a great storm that swept over the British Isles; and in February, 1823, the grand jury at Liverpool called the attention of the magistrates "to the dreadful effects of the late storm . . . in consequence of the modern insecure mode of building." A year later the same body referred again to "the slight and dangerous mode of erecting dwelling houses now practised in this town and neighbourhood" and asked for steps to be taken "to procure a Legislative enactment, which might empower a proper Officer carefully to survey every building hereafter to be erected, and in case of insecurity to cause the danger to be removed."[6]

The sudden collapse of buildings was no new experience. In 1738 Samuel Johnson had written of London as a place where "falling houses thunder on your head"; and, to give a specific instance, in 1796 two houses fell, burying sixteen people, in Houghton Street, where the concrete buildings of the School of Economics now stand.[7] The chief trouble seems to have been the use of inferior material, such as ashes and street sweepings, in the making of bricks and the unsubstantial walls erected whenever the building lease was for only a short run of years.[8] It would appear from the Liverpool evidence, however, that matters had taken a turn for the worse in the early 1820's; and complaints of inferior building in other quarters reinforce the belief. The explanation is not far to seek. It lies in the fact that the early twenties saw a revival of housebuilding after a long period of suspension (or, at best, feeble activity) during nearly a quarter of a century of war and that this revival took place in circumstances when building costs had been raised to an inordinate height.

It is necessary to take account of the organization of the industry. The typical builder was a man of small

6. Sir James A. Picton, *City of Liverpool Archives and Records* (Liverpool: G. G. Walmsley, 1886), pp. 367–68. I am indebted to Dr. W. H. Chaloner for information as to the etymology of "jerry."

7. George, *op. cit.*, p. 73.

8. "The solidity of the building is measured by the duration of the lease, as the shoe by the foot," declared Grosley (*ibid.*, p. 76).

means, a bricklayer or a carpenter, who bought a small plot of land, carried out himself only a single operation, such as that of laying the bricks, and employed craftsmen on contract for the other processes of construction. By the middle of the nineteenth century, it is true, large-scale firms were growing up, controlled by men like Thomas Cubitt, but these were concerned with the erection of public buildings or mansions and not with the dwellings of the poor. The jerry-builders were not, in the usual sense of the word, capitalists but workingmen. Says Chadwick's *Report* of 1842:

In the rural districts, the worst of the new cottages are those erected on the borders of commons by the labourers themselves. In manufacturing districts, the tenements erected by building clubs and by speculating builders of the class of workmen, are frequently the subject of complaint, as being the least substantial and the most destitute of proper accommodation. The only conspicuous instances of improved residences found in the rural districts are those which have been erected by opulent and benevolent landlords for the accommodation of the labourers on their own estates: and in the manufacturing districts, those erected by wealthy manufacturers for the accommodation of their own workpeople.[9]

In Liverpool the builders of so-called "slop houses," or scamped houses, were usually Welshmen, drawn large-

9. *Report on the Sanitary Condition of the Labouring Population of Great Britain* (London, 1842), p. 233. "An immense number of the small houses occupied by the poorer classes in the suburbs of Manchester are of the most superficial character; they are built by members of building clubs, and other individuals, and new cottages are erected with a rapidity that astonishes persons who are unacquainted with their flimsy structure" (*ibid.*, p. 284).

ly from the quarrymen of Caernarvonshire. They were backed by attorneys who had land to dispose of on lease but were not themselves willing to become builders. They bought their materials, which were of a cheap and shoddy type, on three months' credit. They tended to employ a high proportion of apprentices, and so, it was said, workmanship was of low quality.[10] They needed credit at every stage: to obtain the building lease, to purchase the materials, and to meet the claims of the joiners, plasterers, slaters, plumbers, painters, etc., who performed their special tasks as contractors or subcontractors. The price of money was an important element in building costs. Under the operation of the usury laws it was illegal to offer, or demand, more than 5 per cent, and this meant that, at times when the state itself was offering $4\frac{1}{2}$ or more per cent, it was impossible for the builders to obtain loans at all. By allowing the rate of interest to rise to $4\frac{1}{2}$ or 5 per cent on the public debt, and prohibiting the industrialist from offering more, the state had been successful in damping down the activities of the builders for more than twenty years and so had deflected to itself the resources of men and materials required for the prosecution of the war against Napoleon. After 1815 the rate of interest fell tardily; it was not until the early twenties that the builders could resume operations. They were faced with a demand that had swollen enormously as the result of a vast increase of population, which now

10. *Morning Chronicle*, September 16, 1850.

included an abnormally large number of young adults seeking homes of their own.

They were faced also by an enormous increase in costs. In 1821, according to Silberling's index number, wholesale prices in general stood about 20 per cent above the level of the year 1788. In the same period the price of building materials had risen far more: bricks and wainscot had doubled; deals had risen by 60 per cent and lead by 58 per cent. The wages of craftsmen and laborers had gone up by anything from 80 to 100 per cent. The costs of a large number of specific operations are given annually in the *Builders' Price Books* published in London. They show an increase in the cost of plain brickwork of 120 per cent. Oak for building purposes had gone up by 150 per cent, and fir by no less than 237 per cent. The cost of common painting had doubled, and that of glazing with crown glass had increased by 140 per cent.[11]

It was not, in the main, the producer of materials who was responsible. During the war the duties levied by the state on bricks and tiles, stone, slate, and wallpaper had

11. Materials used in the building industry had not been much affected by the changes in industrial technique. The prices of some metal products had, it is true, risen only a little. "Twopenny nails," which cost 1/8*d*. a thousand in 1788, could be had at 1/9*d*. in 1821. Sheet lead had risen only from 22*s*. to 34*s*. per cwt., and solder from 9*d*. to 12*d*. a pound. But "grey stock brick work with good front mortar" had gone up from £9.12*s*. a rod to £18.5*s*.; "oak framed and good" from 2*s*. to 5*s*. a cubic foot, and "glazing with second Newcastle crown glass" from 1/6*d*. to 3/6*d*. a foot.

increased enormously. At this time the cost of timber was the chief element in the total cost of building materials, amounting, according to one estimate, to fully a half of the whole. Almost prohibitive duties had been laid on the supplies of timber and deals from the Baltic, and the builders of working-class houses had to make use of what were generally said to be inferior woods, brought at great cost across the Atlantic from Canada. Joseph Hume declared, in 1850, that, if the duties on bricks and timber were removed, a cottage which cost £60 to build, as things were, could be put up for £40.[12]

All these charges had to come out of rents. But the occupier of a house had to bear further burdens imposed by the state. Windows had been subject to taxation from the time of William III (1696). Before the outbreak of the French wars, all houses paid a fixed rate of 6s. a year and those with seven or more windows additional duties, increasing with the number of windows. There was much stopping-up of lights to avoid the duties. The number of houses chargeable was less in 1798 than in 1750. It is true that the houses of the very poor were excused and that those with fewer than eight windows were exempted in 1825. But these concessions brought no relief to the poor of such cities as London, Newcastle, Edinburgh, and Glasgow, where many of the workers lived in large tenements, which remained liable to the impost. In addition, there was the heavy weight of local

12. Hansard, CVIII, 479 (1850).

taxation. In the case of working-class houses the rates were paid by the landlord but were recovered from the tenants by addition to the rent. Local rates were rising at an alarming rate. Here again, it is true, there were exemptions. It was left to the discretion of the justices of the peace to remit the rates on occupiers who were considered to be too poor to pay them. By the middle of the century about one-third of the houses in the rural counties of Suffolk and Hampshire and one-seventh of those in industrial Lancashire (where poverty was less acute) had been excused the payment of rates.[13] But, it was argued with some force, the exemption was of little benefit to the poor, since it enabled the landlords to charge more for the houses than they would otherwise have done. In any case it led to an increase in the poundage on houses not exempt, and for this reason it was said that "the ratepayers disliked the builders of cottages and thought them public enemies." The odium rested on "Jerry."

In the years that followed the long war, then, the builders had the task of making up arrears of housing and of meeting the needs of a rapidly growing population. They were handicapped by costs, a large part of which arose from fiscal exactions. The expenses of occupying a house were loaded with heavy local burdens, and so the net rent that most workingmen could afford to pay was reduced. In these circumstances, if the rela-

13. *Ibid.*, p. 470 (P. Scrope).

tively poor were to be housed at all, the buildings were bound to be smaller, less substantial, and less well provided with amenities than could be desired.[14] It was emphatically not the machine, not the Industrial Revolution, not even the speculative bricklayer or carpenter that was at fault. Few builders seem to have made fortunes, and the incidence of bankruptcy was high. The fundamental problem was the shortage of houses. Those who blame the jerry-builder remind one of the parson, referred to by Edwin Cannan, who used to upbraid the assembled worshipers for the poor attendance at church.

Stress has rightly been laid by many writers on the inadequacy of the provisions for safeguarding the public against overcrowding of houses on limited sites. But London, Manchester, and other large towns had had their Building Acts for generations,[15] and no one who has looked at the *Builders' Price Books* can possibly believe that Londoners suffered from a deficiency of regulations. Mr. John Summerson, indeed, has suggested that

14. It was estimated that the cost of a working-class house in Liverpool, presumably including the cost of the land, varied in 1850 from £100 to £120 a year and that such a house would let for £12 a year (*Morning Chronicle,* September 16, 1850). A return of 10 or 12 per cent seems high, but it had to cover costs of collection and the risks that the house might be without tenants for part of its life.

15. The first Westminster Paving Act was obtained in 1762; Manchester had an Improvement Act in 1776 and a Police Act in 1792 (Arthur Redford, *A History of Local Government in Manchester* [London and New York: Longmans, Green & Co., 1939–40]). Liverpool's Improvement Acts came in 1785 and 1825.

the depressing monotony of the newer streets of the capital were the direct result, not, as is often assumed, of free enterprise, but of the provisions of what the builders called the Black Act of 1774—a measure that runs to about thirty-five thousand words.[16] It is true that what was uppermost in the minds of those who framed this act was the avoidance of fire. But some writers like the Webbs (as Redford has shown)[17] have done less than justice to the work of the early organs of local government in such matters as the paving, lighting, and cleaning of streets. If more was not done, the fault did not rest on the builders. Thomas Cubitt told the House of Commons that he would not allow a house to be built anywhere unless it could be shown that there was a good drainage and a good way to get rid of water. "I think there should be a public officer paid at the public expense, who should be responsible for that." If the towns were ridden with disease, some at least of the responsibility lay with legislators who, by taxing windows, put a price on light and air and, by taxing bricks and tiles, discouraged the construction of drains and sewers. Those who dwell on the horrors that arose from the fact that the products of the sewers often got mixed up with the drinking water, and attribute this, as all other horrors, to the Industrial Revolution, should be reminded of the

16. John N. Summerson, *Georgian London* (London: Pleiades Book, 1945), p. 108.

17. Redford, *op. cit.*

obvious fact that without the iron pipe, which was one of the products of that revolution, the problem of enabling people to live a healthy life together in towns could never have been solved.[18]

If my first complaint against commonly accepted views of the economic developments of the nineteenth century is concerned with their pessimism, my second is that they are not informed by any glimmering of economic sense. In the generation of Adam Smith and his immediate successors many treatises appeared dealing with the history of commerce, industry, coinage, public revenue, population, and pauperism. Those who wrote them —men like Anderson, Macpherson, Chalmers, Colquhoun, Lord Liverpool, Sinclair, Eden, Malthus, and Tooke—were either themselves economists or at least were interested in the things that were the concern of Adam Smith, Ricardo, and Mill. There were, it is true, many rebels, on both the right and the left, against the doctrines propounded by the economists; but few of these, it so happened, were historically minded. There was, therefore, no sharply defined cleavage between history and theory. In the second half of the nineteenth century, however, a wide breach appeared. How far it was due to the direct influence of the writings of Marx and Engels, how far to the rise of the Historical School of

18. John Wilkinson was supplying iron pipes to the Paris waterworks in 1781, but during the war he and his fellow-ironmasters were making cannon, not pipes. Elm pipes were still being laid down in 1810.

economists in Germany, and how far to the fact that the English economic historians, following Toynbee, were primarily social reformers, I must not stay to discuss. There can be no doubt, however, that the tendency was to write the story in other than economic terms. A whole series of labels was introduced to indicate what were believed to be the dominant characteristics of successive periods of time, and most of these were political rather than economic in connotation. The arresting phrase, the "Industrial Revolution," was coined (as Miss Bezanson has shown)[19] not by English industrialists or economists but by French writers of the late eighteenth century, under the spell of their own great political ferment. It was seized upon by Engels and Marx and was used by Arnold Toynbee as the title of his pioneer work. It may be questioned whether it has not now outlived its usefulness, for it has tended to support the view that the introduction of large-scale production was catastrophic, rather than beneficial, in its effects. Even more unfortunate, I would urge, has been the intrusion into economic history of another phrase of political intent, struck at the same mint but at an even earlier period. Professor Macgregor has traced back the term "laissez faire" to 1755, when it was first used by the Marquis d'Argenson

19. Anne Bezanson, "The Early Use of the Term 'Industrial Revolution,'" *Quarterly Journal of Economics*, XXXVI, No. 2 (February, 1922), 343.

as both a political and an economic principle.[20] He has charted its curious evolution from the time when it meant noninterference with industry to its use, in 1907, by Alfred Marshall to mean "let the State be up and doing." In view of the dubiety of its intention, it is perhaps not to be wondered at that it should have been fastened by some onto a period of English history that is known to others as the Age of Reform—again a phrase drawn from the vocabulary of politics and not of economics. One could not feel too harshly, therefore, about the candidate who declared that "about the year 1900 men turned their backs on laissez-faire and began to do things for themselves." The title of a work written by Mr. Fisher Unwin in 1904 has fastened on the decade that saw the railway boom and the repeal of the Corn Laws the stigma of "the hungry forties," and only the other day a magazine called *Womanfare* referred to the decade before the recent war as "the hungry thirties." A legend is growing up that the years 1930–39 were marked throughout by misery. In the next generation "the hungry thirties" may be common form.

For two generations economic historians have shirked economic questions or have dealt with them superficially. They have never made up their minds on such elementary matters as to whether it is abundance or scarcity that is to be sought, but generally it is restrictionism they

20. D. H. Macgregor, *Economic Thought and Policy* (London, 1949).

favor. The efforts of Lancashire to provide cheap cottons for people who had previously gone seminaked is acknowledged only in a sentence to the effect that "the bones of the cotton weavers whitened the plains of India." In the same elementary textbook I am told that the tax on imports of wheat led to poverty and distress in the first half of the nineteenth century and that the absence of such a tax to act as a dam against the flood of cheap wheat that poured across the Atlantic was the prime cause of the poverty and distress of the later decades of the century—the period so unhappily known as the Great Depression. Some economic historians have written chapters designed to answer such questions as to whether trade arises from industry or industry from trade, whether transport develops markets or markets give occasion for transport. They have concerned themselves with inquiries as to where the demand comes from that makes production possible. Whenever a real problem is encountered, it is passed over with some such comment as that "a crisis arose" or that "speculation became rife," though why or what nature is rarely disclosed. And, when details are given, logic is often thrown to the winds. In explaining the French depression of 1846, Professor Clough declares that "reduced agricultural production lowered the purchasing power of the farmers, and the high cost of living prevented the industrial population from buying much else than food." This surely is a case of making the worst of both worlds.

It has often been said that, at least before Keynes, the economic theorist moved in a world of abstractions and had nothing worth while to offer the historian. But, if only historians had pondered a little on marginal analysis, they would have been saved from such foolish assertions as that trade can arise only when there is a surplus or that investment abroad takes place only when the capital market at home is sated. Ignorance of the elements of economic theory led historians to give political interpretations to every favorable trend. In scores of books the improvement in conditions of labor in the nineteenth century has been attributed to factory legislation; in hardly any is it pointed out that rising productivity of male labor had something to do with the decline of the number of children exploited in the factories or the number of women degraded in the mines. Until Professor Rostow wrote his work on the *British Economy of the Nineteenth Century* in 1948, there had been scarcely any discussion by historians of the relation between investment and earnings.

No one has laid more stress on the need for theory in the writing of history than Sombart. "Facts are like beads," he declares; "they require a string to hold them together. . . . No theory—no history." It is to be deplored that he found his own theory, not in the writings of the economists of his day, but in those of Karl Marx; for, although later he reacted strongly against the interpretations of Marx, his writings have led large numbers of historians in Germany, Britain, and the United States to thread their facts on a Marxist string. In particular, everything that has happened, since the early Middle Ages, is explained in terms of capitalism—a term if not coined at least given wide currency by Marx. Marx, of course, associated it with exploitation. Sombart used it to mean a system of production differing from the handicraft system by reason of the fact that the means of production are owned by a class distinct from the workers—a class whose motive is profit and whose methods are rational, as opposed to the traditional methods, of the handicraftsmen. Above all, he stressed the capitalist spirit. Other elements, such as that innovations in the system are carried out by borrowed money, or credit, have been added by later writers like Schumpeter. But nearly all agree that capitalism implies the existence of a rational technique, a proletariat that sells its labor (and not the product of its labor), and a class of capitalists whose aim is unlimited profit. The assumption is that at some stage of human history—perhaps in the eleventh century A.D.—men became, for the first time, rational and acquisitive. The main business of the economic historians who followed Sombart was to trace the origins of rationality and acquisitiveness. It was what they called the "genetic approach" to the problem of capitalism.

A thousand years is an unmanageably long period, and so capitalism had to be presented as a series of stages —the epochs, respectively, of early, full, and late capitalism, or of mercantile capitalism, industrial capitalism, finance capitalism, and state capitalism. It is admitted, of course, by those who make use of these categories that there is overlapping: that the late stage of one epoch is the early (or, as they say, the emergent) stage of the next. But to teach economic history in this way— to suggest that commerce, industry, finance, and state control are *successive* dominant forces—is to hide from the student, I suggest, the interaction and interdependence of all these at every period of time. It is bad economics.

Those who write so tend to torture the facts. It is part of the legend that the dominant form of organization under industrial capitalism, the factory, arose out of the demands, not of ordinary people, but of the rich and the rulers. Let me quote Professor Nussbaum here. "In personal terms," he says, "it was the interests of the princes [the state] and of the industrialists; in impersonal terms, war and luxury favoured—one might almost say, caused—the development of the factory system." To support this monstrous thesis, he gives a list of the capitalized industries about the year 1800. It includes "sugar, chocolate, lace, embroidery, novelties, tapestries, mirrors, porcelains, jewellery, watches and book printing."[21] All I can say is that, apart from that of sugar, I cannot find a single instance of the production

21. Fredrick L. Nussbaum, *A History of the Economic Institution of Modern Europe* (New York: F. S. Crofts & Co., 1933), p. 334.

of any one of these things in a factory in England at this time.[22] Nussbaum admits that cotton clothes "offered a field for almost exclusively capitalistic organisation" but says that this was because they were "at first and for a long time luxury goods." Apparently he thinks Arkwright and his fellows were making fine muslins and cambrics for royal courts and not calicoes for English workers and the peasants of India. But this legend about war and luxury is too absurd to need refutation by anyone who has taken the trouble to glance at the records of the first generation of factory masters in England.

The truth is (as Professor Koebner has said) that neither Marx nor Sombart (nor, for that matter, Adam Smith) had any idea of the real nature of what we call the Industrial Revolution. They overstressed the part played by science and had no conception of an economic system that develops spontaneously without the help of either the state or the philosopher. It is, however, the stress on the capitalist spirit that has, I think, done most harm. For, from being a phrase suggesting a mental or emotional attitude, it has became an impersonal, super-human force. It is no longer men and women, exercising free choice, who effect change, but capitalism, or the

22. As a piece of reasoning it may be set alongside the statement of Nussbaum (*ibid.*, p. 251) that a shortage of ore and fuel in the iron industry of the eighteenth century "led characteristically to high costs of production, therefore to a narrowing of the market, hence to still higher costs and in general to a sharp limitation of the development of the capitalistic organisation."

spirit of capitalism. "Capitalism," says Schumpeter, "develops rationality." "Capitalism exalts the monetary unit." "Capitalism produced the mental attitude of modern science." "Modern pacificism, modern international morality, modern feminism, are products of capitalism." Whatever this is, it is certainly not economic history. It has introduced a new mysticism into the recounting of plain facts. What am I to do with a candidate who purports to explain why the limited-liability company came into being in England in the 1850's in the following words? I quote literally from the scripture: "Individualism was forced to give way to laissez faire as the development of capitalism found the early emergent stage of entrepreneurial capitalism a hindrance to that rational expansive development which is the very ethos of capitalism."

Sombart, Schumpeter, and their followers are concerned with final, rather than efficient, causes. Even so austere a historian as Professor Pares has been infected. "Capitalism itself causes," he writes, "to some extent the production of commercial crops, because it demands a payment in some currency that can be realised at home."[23] The point of view is *ex post* rather than *ex ante*. Of the genetic approach in general, Professor Gras has well said: "It takes facts out of their setting. In emphasizing the genesis or evolution, it implies an original im-

23. Bernard Pares, "The Economic Factors in the History of the Empire," *Economic History Review*, VII, No. 2 (May, 1927).

pulse, which, once started, carried on to the end." In other words, things happen because capitalism requires them to happen—even, it may be added, to an end not yet reached. "A socialist form of society will inevitably emerge from an equally inevitable decomposition of capitalist society," wrote Schumpeter. It may be so. But I do not want to see history written as though its function were simply to exhibit the gradualness of inevitability.

I do not wish to leave the impression that I am disrespectful of Sombart and Schumpeter. Against their massive achievements my own small contributions to economic history must appear as the fumbling of an amateur. But I hold strongly that the future of the subject lies in closer co-operation with the work of economists and that phrases which perhaps served a purpose a generation ago should now be discarded. One of the best historical vindications of American economic civilization has been written, within Sombart's framework, by Professor Hacker. I can only express the opinion that it would have lost little, if any, of its brilliance, and would have been equally convincing, if it had been presented entirely in Professor Hacker's own lucid words. Above all, I do not believe that the centuries have held nothing but cruelty and exploitation. I believe, with George Unwin, that it is from the spontaneous actions and choices of ordinary people that progress—if I may use an anachronistic word—springs and that it is not true that everything rolls on to a predetermined end under the dynamics (whatever that means) of an impersonal force known as capitalism. I believe that the creative achievements of the state have been vastly overrated and that, in the words of Calvin Coolidge, "where the people are the government they do not get rid of their burdens by attempting to unload them on the government." Looking around me, I feel that men are learning by bitter experience the truth of those words. I used to cherish the hope that the study of history might save us from having to learn that way. If I have stressed what seem to me to be the illogical and illiberal tendencies of some of my colleagues, I must end by saying that I am heartened by the knowledge that at the School of Economics and elsewhere in Britain and America there is growing up a body of young teachers who are not antagonistic to economic ways of thought and to liberal ideas. I do not believe that what I regard as the citadels of error will yield to any frontal attack. But I do believe that there are, both in scholarship and in the world of action, forces stirring that give promise of better things.

2

The Anticapitalist Bias of
American Historians

LOUIS M. HACKER

I am addressing myself to the same theme that has attracted the attention of Professor Ashton. In the first part of my paper I comment on the general significance of the ideas he examines; in the second, I discuss the present attitude of American historians toward capitalism.

I

This is the kind of thoughtful presentation one has learned to expect from Ashton, for he has that rare quality among economic historians of being able to see both the whole and its parts clearly. None has given us a set of more illuminating pictures of the detailed development of industrial enterprise in Britain; none has succeeded as happily as he in presenting a general philosophical view of the character and significance of the nineteenth century in economic—or I should say, rather, in political economic—terms. It is fashionable to-day (more so, indeed, than it was a generation ago when the authority of the Webbs and the Hammonds went un-

challenged) to traduce the nineteenth century. Charles
A. Beard[1] in America and E. H. Carr[2] in England, to
name the most prominent, again and again insist upon its
moral failure. It concerned itself with making money
(through cheap goods, of course, but even the word
"cheap" is invested with a sinister connotation), but it
lost sight of those deeper values which, presumably,
gave earlier times a direction and inner meaning. The
nineteenth century had no sense of responsibility, and, in
its pursuit of material possessions, it materialized, or
vulgarized, common attitudes. Not only does our world
lack unity; it lacks purpose and confidence. It is assumed
that the eighteenth century possesed them and that it is
not too late for the twentieth century to recapture them.

Ashton is so right in protesting against current efforts
to romanticize our preindustrial world, as Boissonnade[3]
so effectively stripped bare all the pretensions of those
who were seeking to pretty up the medieval world. I
myself have tried to raise the alarm against the assumption that preindustrial Europe had a moral attitude to-

1. Charles A. and Mary R. Beard, *The Rise of American Civilization* (2 vols.; New York: Macmillan Co., 1927) ; *America in Mid-
passage* (New York: Macmillan Co., 1939) ; *The American Spirit:
A Study of the Idea of Civilization in the United States* (New York:
Macmillan Co., 1942).

2. Edward H. Carr, *Conditions of Peace* (New York: Macmillan
Co., 1942) ; *The Soviet Impact on the Western World* (New York:
Macmillan Co., 1947).

3. P. Boissonnade, *Life and Work in Medieval Europe,* trans.
Eileen Power (New York: A. A. Knopf, 1927).

ward its laboring populations.[4] Quite the reverse: if the lives of the great majority—before the nineteenth century—were brutish, nasty, and short (under the manorial system, under the cottage system, under American plantation slavery), it is exactly because, despite the alleged securities of status and custom, there was no interest in betterment. There is no meaner attitude toward human nature than is to be found in the moralists of the eighteenth century (I cite Defoe and Mandeville) who regarded men as incapable of achieving their own salvation.[5] Men needed a superior authority—of custom, law, and punishment—in order to maintain that prescription which assured internal balances; today we call that authority "social planning." Both attitudes essentially distrust the capacities of men, exercising their intelligence, to order their lives harmoniously.

The common charge of inhumanity against the nineteenth century—for that is the popular reading of the policy of laissez faire, is it not?—would be an idle slander if it were not so gross. On three counts at least the indictment is false. The nineteenth century, for the first

4. L. M. Hacker, *Shaping of the American Tradition* (2 vols.; New York: Columbia University Press, 1947); *England and America—The Ties That Bind: An Inaugural Lecture* (Oxford: Clarendon Press, 1948).

5. See the excellent discussion on this point in E. S. Furniss, *The Position of the Laborer in a System of Nationalism* (Boston: Houghton Mifflin Co., 1920). Curiously enough Heckscher's great work on mercantilism and Keynes, who follows his quite slavishly, avoid quite entirely the moral implications of mercantilist doctrine.

time, introduced on a broad scale the state policies of public health and public education. The nineteenth century, by turning out cheap goods, made possible the amazing climb of real wages in industrialized economies. The nineteenth century, by permitting the transfer of capital in large amounts, opened up the interiors of backward countries for development and production. For we must not forget that the investments of trading companies, before the nineteenth century, rarely penetrated beyond the seacoasts themselves. Early investments did not lead to capital improvements on a significant scale; the maintenance of trading stations did little to increase the production or transport systems of the peoples being reached and therefore the marginal productivity of their labor. The record of Britain in America and India, before the nineteenth century, is clear on this point, as is, indeed, that of France. One exception is to be noted in the West Indies, and that is in the case of plantation wares. But certainly it is plain that British and French capital did not move overseas to any important degree into manufactures, internal transport, and banking until the nineteenth century.

Ashton has shown why, in the first half of the nineteenth century in Britain, at any rate, there were obstacles to greater improvement than might have occurred. The extraordinary burgeoning of the towns was one of the characteristics of industrialization. It was difficult for private investment to keep pace with housing demand;

hence those wretched slums and jerry-built houses of which social reformers have been so eloquent in their denunciation. Ashton has pointed out that artificially maintained interest rates and an unsound fiscal policy placed obstacles in the way of risk capital. We must not forget, too, that the great expansion of towns was furthered because of the renewal of the inclosure movement, the heavy Irish immigration, and the decline in the death rate. Obviously, none of these had the sinister connotations of exploitation that the critics of the factory system were prepared to discover. This is what I mean when I commend Ashton for his great insights in handling what might appear to be unimportant details. The tax on windows affected the character of urban multiple dwellings; the excises on building materials made costs high. Poor houses and overcrowding in the towns were not evidences of a rejection of moral responsibility on the part of the new industrial class but the result of natural forces of immigration and internal population movements and bad fiscal policy.

At this point Ashton deals the exploitation theory of the Marxians and the Fabians a heavy blow. Ashton is equally realistic in his critical handling of the broad genetic interpretation of the Marxians and Sombartians. He is afraid that a theoretical analysis of economic development in capitalist terms is of little use; perhaps the contrary. It should be recalled that, for dialectical purposes, Marx and Engels found it imperative to divide the economic history of mankind into a series of stages, all linked by dialectical law. Classical slavery was transformed into manorial serfdom, and this in turn into factory exploitation, through the operations of immutable dialectical principles. Each in an early stage was progressive (how, then, account for Greek science and philosophy, Roman law, and medieval art?); each became exploitative, and the seeds of its own destruction took root and grew. Revolution broke out—through the negation of the negation—and society was ready for another and uneasy climb toward the sun and freedom. All those stages were preliminary to the final struggle for and realization of socialism; but they had to develop in orderly fashion. To this extent, Marx and Engels were the children of Newton and Hegel. Darwin perilously shook their mechanically ordered universe.

In the Marxian analysis these forces and challenges—thesis, antithesis, synthesis—were wholly material and were to be found entirely in the relations of production. All else in society—morality, law, art, social relations—was "superstructure." And morality, law, and art could have no independent life or sanctions of their own. There was one other curious shortcoming of the Marxian reading of history: feudalism was transformed into capitalism (i.e., industrial capitalism) by dialectical change. But what of the great trading epoch of western Europe that was developing simultaneously in the cities of Italy, southern Germany, Flanders, and France during the twelfth to eighteenth centuries? This was "merchant capital" or "usury capital"; it was nonproductive and in the Marxian phrase lived in the interstices of and upon a productive society. One of the most shocking things Marx did was his pamphlet on the Jews in which he explained (and by implication justified) anti-Semitism because the Jews were "usury" and "merchant" capitalists.

Here, Ashton is right; the stage or genetic analysis of Marx not only is wrong but has brought incalculable suffering to the world. The fault, it should be pointed out, is the linking of a stage theory with the dialectic and with the theory of "superstructure." This makes this view of economic development deterministic and fatalistic.

Ashton equally is on firm ground in rejecting Sombart. Sombart sought to overcome the inadequacies and fill in the great lacunae of Marx. He saw stages in capitalist development: merchant capitalism, industrial capitalism, finance (or high) capitalism, state (or late) capitalism. Capitalism was characterized by spirit, which was rationalistic, acquisitive, planful. When the capitalist spirit declined, capitalism moved into another stage as a result of a new rationality. Hence, merchant capital moved into industrial capital because of the requirements of the luxury and war-making industries, these two great props and interests of the seventeenth and eighteenth centuries absolute monarchies. Sombart, writing economic history and renouncing Marx, as the successive editions of his *Socialism and the Social Movement in the Nineteenth Century* revealed, did not surrender Hegel. He rejected dialectical materialism but not dialectical idealism. If the spirit was to rule the universe by dialectical law and if Naziism heralded a rebirth of the Teutonic spirit—now that finance capitalism had run its course—then Naziism had historical justification on its side. So, as the Marxian stage analysis brought us inevitably to communism, the Sombartian stage theory brought us to the Third Reich and its one thousand years of glory.

Ashton would be the first to agree that Marx and Sombart made outstanding contributions to economic history; I would be the first to agree that their philosophies of history were errant and dangerous nonsense. However, a stage analysis of economic change has its uses, just as its oversimplification has many pitfalls. We know, at the time that the manorial system ruled on the land and the Italian merchants were establishing trading relations with the Byzantine and Moslem worlds, German capitalists were setting up the coal-mining industry—with the heavy capital outlays such enterprise required. Here we have, in stage terms, feudalism, merchant capitalism, and industrial capitalism side by side. We know that, at the time the great trading companies were flourishing in Britain in the seventeenth century, many small producers—without the benefit of joint stocks—were already developing the coal and iron, building materials, and other industrial enterprises. We know that in America, in the early twentieth century, when presumably finance capitalists in the persons of the Morgans, Rockefellers, and the like were dominating industrial enterprise, the great automobile industry was developing out of the experiments and risks and failures of literally hundreds of small enterprisers.

Yet a stage analysis—as I have pursued it in my *Triumph of American Capitalism*[6] and subsequently— can throw real light on economic change. But such an analysis cannot be dialectical or deterministic (in Marxian terms) or dialectical or rationalistic (in Sombartian terms). Thus, in talking of American events, it would be bad history to leave out the theories of empire and law developed in Colonial America in seeking to account for the American Revolution. It cannot be done in terms of the rejection of the mercantilist system entirely. And, in discussing the American Civil War, it would be fatal to leave out the great role played by abolitionism, which made slavery out to be an immoral way of life. The conflict between the agrarian capitalism of the South and the thwarted industrial capitalism of the North is only part of the story.

But a stage analysis also throws great light on changes in public policy; and I submit that economic history is a twice-told but an incomplete tale unless there is con-

6. New York: Simon & Schuster, 1940.

stant attention being paid to the role of the state—as a hindering or a fostering agency. To this extent, the idea of laissez faire is a fiction. For the state, by negative action—that is, by refusing to adopt certain policies— can affect economic events just as significantly as when its intervention occurs. Ashton himself gives an important example. We know that in Britain the woolen industry, from at least the sixteenth century on, although the Elizabethan Statute of Labourers has its origins in medieval times, labored under many heavy restrictions. The Crown did not extend these to the cotton industry; and it was no accident that great industrial advances took place in this sector so early. Similarly, in America, from 1836 to 1913, all federal interest in central banking policy was abandoned, and this negative attitude on the part of the American government had profound effects on American economic development.

I want to say more than this in defense of the stage analysis as I am employing the term. I think it will be admitted that, at certain points in a nation's historical development, one group or another's interests become predominant and articulate. Then public policy, for good or ill, takes shape. In Britain, before the 1830's and 1840's, the dominant economic interest was a trading or merchant one, as opposed to an industrial interest. Public policy, in consequence, was hostile or at best indifferent to the requirements of the rising industrial enterprisers. It is no accident that in the 1830's and

1840's so many of the remnants of the old system were swept out, as the industrialists increasingly made their power felt. The Reform Act, Corn Law repeal, the final termination of the Acts of Trade and Navigation, thoroughgoing fiscal reform ending in Gladstone's triumph, a reordering of the country's banking system, a new Company's Act, a new organic law for the overseas possessions—can one say that all these are not the measure of the coming-of-age in Britain of its industrial capitalist class? Ashton comments on the fact that the economists of the period were constantly concerning themselves with public questions; that is, they were political economists. Small wonder, in the light of the extraordinary new requirements being imposed on the state in an age of transition.

Or take another example from American history. From the 1830's to 1860, the dominant economic interest in the United States was the agrarian slave-capitalist group of the South. The maintenance of its economy was linked with free trade, cheap navigation costs, easy money or an absence of central banking, and low taxation. It was opposed to protective tariffs, government subsidy of oceanic transportation and railroads, federal supervision of banking, easy immigration, etc. But those who looked to the industrial conversion of the American economy needed public assistance in all these areas; and it was no accident that the Republican party wrote almost all these measures into law during the years

1861–65, when the Civil War was raging. In other words, a description of the American economy during the years 1830–60 in terms of the antagonism between the planters and their merchant allies, on the one hand, and the young industrialists, on the other, throws a flood of light on the effort to maintain or change drastically state policy.

Economic history, in consequence, must be many things. It must study more sensitively than it has the impact of political theory (Locke, Harrington, Montesquieu), moral ideas (Wilberforce, the American Abolitionists), and fiscal policy on changes in production and consumption. Indeed, I would say that central to its problems are those of risk-taking and fiscal policy, and the two mesh at so many points that to separate them would be futile and unreal. I think, too, that the term "capitalism" is an important one and that it should not only be retained but defended. We must clear away the rubble that has accumulated on this ancient citadel since Marx and Engels and Sombart wrote. As in the case of the excavations of Troy, only patience and devotion will permit us to triumph in the end. And the rubble is so heavy: dialectical revolution, rationalistic spirit, human exploitation, personal greed—all the cant, fury, and misguided sentiment of one hundred years! The digging is worth our efforts, for at the bottom we shall find a system and a set of attitudes which have made possible material progress and the alleviation of human suffering.

This system and attitudes we may as well call "capitalism"; and if we define it, for historical analysis, as the risk-taking function of private individuals (who, by the process—if they are successful—create capital) and the development and maintenance of sound fiscal policy by the state, I think we will be able to save the term from the opprobrium from which it suffers.

II

So much for a general analysis. Where do American historians, at the present moment, stand as regards the role of capitalism in their country's development? Generally, it may be said, one notes an anticapitalist bias. But in the United States, at any rate, the anticapitalist bias of many of its historians is not necessarily due to Marxist influences. Marxian ideas have played a role, but their impact has been light and brief. When I say "Marxian," I should differentiate between two aspects of the doctrine—that which was sifted through the nonrevolutionary lenses of Fabianism or Social Democracy and that which came through the harsher, or revolutionary, analysis of Lenin. Some young Americans interested in history were converted to Marxism by way of the *Imperialism* and *State and Revolution* and, in consequence, learned to think dialectically. But of this later.

American historical writing, up to the second half of the 1920's, it may be said generally, gave little attention to economics in the theoretical sense. Not only was there no effort to interpret historical events in a broad economic context (Weber, Sombart, Sée, and Pirenne were unknown or, if read and commented on, appeared only in sociological literature); there was no interest in or understanding of the parts played by central banking, capital transfers, and capital formation in the country's development. When economic data were adduced—as in McMaster's *History of the American People*—they were as social history or as institutional inventions or changes. Such American historians discussed the transportation systems, the coming of manufactures, the condition of the working and farming classes, but only in passing. For American historians were largely interested in political and military history; and they wrote of the unfolding of the American story almost entirely in nationalist (i.e., isolationist) terms. There were certain grand themes, quite unique to America, that inevitably caught their interest: the conquest of a virgin continent and the frontier's effect on political institutions and social habits; the unending stream—up to 1920—of the Europeans who in America sought escape from the Old World's inequalities; the recurring struggle between Jeffersonian and Hamiltonian ideas—that is, the creation and maintenance of a weak or a strong central authority; the intrusion of moral questions into the American public debates—slavery, women's rights, prohibition. These themes were never treated in general or universal economic terms or in their relations to Europe; indeed,

the allegedly essential character of America's history—
that it was taking place in isolation—was rarely questioned.

Charles A. Beard's *The Rise of American Civilization,*
first published in 1927, had a powerful influence on
younger writers particularly with the onset of the Great
Depression. *The Rise of American Civilization,* in effect,
was the projection on a vast screen of the ideas with
which Beard had experimented in little as early as 1913.
In the earlier year Beard had written *An Economic Interpretation of the American Constitution;* in this *tour
de force* Beard showed no familiarity with European
economic historians starting with Marx; in fact, he in-
sisted that a reading of Madison's Tenth Paper of the
Federalist was enough to furnish the ideological basis of
his analysis. And, in a sense, Beard was on firm ground.
He was no determinist by any Marxian or Sombartian
reading; he was prepared simply to take the position
that men's direct financial interests had immediate effects
on the political decisions they helped to shape. Thus, a
large number of the members of the Constitutional Convention of 1787 were men of property; they were merchants or land speculators or held government stock.
Hence, it was natural that they should seek protection
of their property rights in the creation of a strong central government. The broader economic implications of
such a position—notably the implications of policy
founded on such a base in respect to the establishment

and possibilities of survival of a new country—Beard was not prepared to examine. Nor was Beard willing to take sides: for or against the assumption of the state debts; for or against the creation of a central banking scheme; for or against the protection of infant industries. Presumably he was engaged in objective historical analysis; it never occurred to him that his work had a fatal flaw. Even assuming the wealth of some of the members of the Constitutional Convention, it was a major error to take for granted (by silence on the point) that public policy, as well as private interest, was not also their close concern.

In *The Rise of American Civilization*—on a broader canvas, for Beard was now writing the history of the United States—the essential Beard emerged. At least at three points in American history Beard saw the influence of economic forces: in the American revolt against Britain, in the struggle over slavery leading up to the Civil War, and in the Republican party's triumph in the years 1865–96. It was when he came to the last—the writing of the Fourteenth Amendment, the drafting of tariff legislation, the "spoliation" of the country's natural resources, and the defeat of the organized farmers politically and economically—that Beard's own moral sanctions were set out. "The Gilded Age" or "The Great Barbecue" was the awful price the United States was called upon to pay for the victory of the Republican partly and the emerging group of industrial capitalists for which it spoke: in class stratification and exploitation, in the piling-up of huge fortunes by evil means, in the vulgarization of taste. This was America's turning point; and, despite its growing economic power and its increasing demand for recognition in world affairs, it parted with its heritage and its promise.

In the last volume of his series of four, in which Beard examined the meaning of the idea of civilization in America, he came to the conclusion that its Golden Age was not that of Concord—of the Transcendentalists, the Abolitionists, the early advocates of public education and women's rights—but that of the eighteenth-century Enlightenment—a world of order, light, and abstract justice. His composite of the American eighteenth-century *philosophes* was like Michelangelo's Moses: larger than life, more divine than human, immobile and perfect. And his composite hero—an elegant Jefferson combining all the virtues of Montesquieu and Condorcet—moved in a rarefied world of high thinking about abstract rights; into this formal Garden of Eden petty politics, political compromise, and the business of the market place never grossly intruded.

I talk of Charles A. Beard at some length because I regard him as a major force in accounting for the anticapitalist bias to be found in much of recent American historical writing. Beard, in effect, took over the agrarian prejudices of his own Indiana boyhood to the capitalist processes. Late in life he found a remote and mechanical justification for his dislikes. He never showed an interest in these capitalist processes as such or in their economic consequences; but he rejected both for moral rather than for class, ideological, or dialectical reasons. In his own writings and in those he influenced, in consequence, no effort is made to analyze or comprehend the contributions of capitalism to America's extraordinary growth.

Somewhat akin to the position taken by Beard—that is, rejection on moral grounds—was that of Gustavus Myers, whose *History of the Great American Fortunes* appeared in 1909. Myers was a social democrat in the tradition of Bernstein, Jaurès, and the Fabians. He preached the coming of the socialist commonwealth; but he did not do so in dialectical or revolutionary terms. Capitalism was evil and had to be replaced, at the polls, by democratic socialism. In consequence his major work is a miscellany of anecdotes, half-true tales, and uncritically handled court records of the plunderings and self-aggrandizement of those who built America's great fortunes, whether on the land, in trade, or in the railroad industries. Peculation, fraud, and theft largely were their instruments; their fortunes were ill-gotten gains, and a society which disinherited their heirs would be performing an act of historical justice. Myers was a classic of socialist literature and as such known to a small company of the elect; but in 1934, with the publication of Josephson's *The Robber Barons*[7] (almost entirely based on Myers), his influence became pervasive. These attitudes, in particular, one may trace to Myers-Josephson or a combination of Beard-Myers: (1) that great fortunes in America were built up by fraud; (2) that the country's natural resources were looted in the process; and (3) that the social consequences of private ownership and wealth were unhappy—in creating classes, in subordinating agriculture, in building slums, etc.

These anticapitalist influences were not Leninist (i.e., dialectical). A small group of American historians, affiliated openly with the Communist party or sympathetic to it, beginning with the 1930's, began to write American history in dialectical terms.[8] Following Lenin, they saw capitalism in its death throes; and its final agonies were revealed in the uneasy threat of world war and in colonial restiveness. The classical Leninist model was employed: of a capitalist society becoming more rigid because of monopolist concentration; of working-class exploitation; of the deepening of the business cycle. All American history, as a result, was a preparation for the great fifth act, when revolution would destroy a society already rot-

7. Matthew Josephson, *The Robber Barons* (New York: Harcourt, Brace & Co., 1934).

8. An interesting example of this kind of writing is P. S. Foner, *History of the Labor Movement in the United States* (New York: International Publishers, 1947).

ten to the core and permit the class-conscious proletariat to capture power.

These were curious and frequently amusing exercises, written in the stiff jargon of Lenin and utilizing a set of tools of analysis so alien to the vocabulary and thinking of Americans that few outside the Communist party read these works. It may be said that, unlike the fields of creative writing, Communist influences on historical work were slight. In brief, I am saying that the anti-capitalist bias in American history does not stem from Communist (i.e., dialectical) sources.

Having described the effects of the thinking of Beard and Myers, one has not recorded the whole story. The anticapitalism of a good part of American historical writing really has its basis in a political discussion which has a perennial attraction for American writers of history. To put it simply—certainly too simply—this revolves about the struggle between Hamiltonianism and Jeffersonianism. That Americans come back to this theme again and again should not surprise Europeans. In their own historical literatures there are also traditions that have an unending fascination: in France there is Jacobinism; in Britain, left-wing Protestantism.

The conflict between Hamiltonianism and Jeffersonianism must not be viewed too naïvely; it is more than a debate over the structure of the state (strong versus weak central government) and more than a disagreement over the question of state intervention (all or none).

Intervention in whose interest is part of the problem as well as intervention for what purpose. In almost every instance where the question obtrudes, it is viewed from the viewpoint of pure politics; that is, moral issues are involved. Here one differentiates, obviously, between politics, on the one hand, and political economy, on the other.

In recent years the anticapitalist bias of American historians, it may be said, stems from their espousal of Jeffersonian as opposed to Hamiltonian ideas. This is a current phenomenon; in fact, until twenty or so years ago, interest in Jefferson was slight. He has emerged from relative obscurity for a number of reasons—all of which have to do with the question which Americans today seek to answer. Jefferson as the champion of natural rights (for natural today read "human"); Jefferson as the spokesman for equalitarianism; Jefferson as the foe of an established church; Jefferson, notably, who sought to challenge "monopoly"—this is the advocate whose words (not deeds) are being invoked. And because those who challenged him or his ideas (or their extension) frequently were associated with capitalist institutions or policy, those historians who seek inspiration in Jefferson or Jeffersonianism are anticapitalists. One should note, too, of course, the broad implications of Jefferson's attack on "monopoly"; only in the wide diffusion of property ownership (i.e., wealth) could social stability and economic progress be found.

There are at least five points, in historical studies, in recent years, where Jefferson or Jeffersonians are favored against those who took opposite views. Let me note these briefly.

1. In a re-examination of the story of the founding of the Republic, that is to say, the years immediately following the American Revolution, historians are seeking to argue that the efforts to erect a strong central government during 1787–89 disregarded the already tangible achievements of the thirteen sovereign states to create stability. Forces were at work to overcome the initial chaos; and a working federation would have emerged capable of resolving the pressing problems of trade, monetary questions, and international relations. But Federalism (i.e., Hamiltonian ideas) won the day, partly by duress and fraud, and the consequences were dire. The establishment of a Supreme Court to override the legislative will and the acceptance of the idea of implied powers in the central government were some of the political results. And because the Federalists (i.e., Hamiltonians) pressed for a central government, all their works must be under a cloud. A sound monetary system, a central bank, the credit-worthiness of the new republic, support of infant industries—the essential heart of the Hamiltonian political economic program—must be rejected along with Hamilton's antidemocratic and antipluralistic ideas. It is important to observe that the economics of Hamiltonism—that is to say, the public

policy a new and underdeveloped country was to follow in a world where the great powers (France Spain, Britain) constantly threatened—is never analyzed as such. Politically, to these leveling historians, Hamiltonism was evil; and by the same token a moral and not an economic judgment is passed on his extraordinary achievements.[9]

2. The same viewpoint rules in the rewriting of the history of the Jacksonian period. Jackson, himself a man of wealth and a slaveowner, became a leveling Jeffersonian; he sought to speak for the common man, notably challenging the power of the central government. His political opponents, the Whigs, once more invoking Hamiltonian ideas, hoped to employ the central government for the installation of a political economic program made up of protective tariffs, central banking, and public aid for internal improvements. Jackson raised the cry of "monopoly" and was successful. The Whigs were routed and their program defeated. Politics, instead of preoccupying itself with economic questions for the next generation, sought escape in expansionism. The slavery question boiled underneath and in 1860 finally erupted. Enough to say that the historians sympathetic to Jackson are also anticapitalist. That a protective tariff, a sound monetary system, and a government plan of public works

9. See Merrill Jensen, *The New Nation: A History of the United States during the Confederation, 1781–1785* (New York: A. A. Knopf, 1950); Dumas Malone, *Jefferson and the Rights of Man* (Boston: Little, Brown & Co., 1951).

might have hastened industrialization and therefore automatically ended slavery is beside the point. The Whigs were antilevelers and strong-government men; and, again, their economic ideas must be rejected.[10]

3. The recent defense of the slavery system as a moral society—J. G. Randall explicitly takes this position, and here he is followed by almost all present-day American historians writing on the preliminaries leading up to the Civil War—has resulted in a campaign of calumny against its foes. The opponents of the South made up a mixed company: some were Abolitionists, some were levelers, some were the rising company of young industrialists who saw in a revival of Hamiltonian ideas the salvation of the Republic. Because the slavery advocates were also states' rights men (the only remnants of Jeffersonianism surviving), their defenders today are prepared to condemn the economic ideas as well as the political doctrine of the Radical Republicans. Curiously enough, the reconstruction program of the Abolitionists (for political and social equality for the Negroes) is rejected, as is also their economic plans. In Hamiltonianism, Whiggism, and Republicanism there is to be found the same strain—the intervention of government to assure monetary stability and economic progress. A protective tariff system, a national banking program, government support of railroads, homesteads for farmers, easy

10. See A. M. Schlesinger, Jr., *The Age of Jackson* (Boston: Little, Brown & Co., 1945).

immigration—only in detail did the founders of the Republican party differ from the Federalists and the Whigs.[11]

4. Organized farmers challenged the new industrialists in the generation after the Civil War. The farmers—in debt and confronted by falling prices (although the prices of agricultural staples did not drop so sharply as did those of steel, oil products, and textiles)—turned bitterly against the Republican party and all its works. They raised the banners of People's Land, People's Money, and People's Transportation. By the first, they sought the ousting of foreign owners of great grazing tracts and the seizure of unpatented lands of the land-grant railroads (most of which were owned abroad). By the second, they meant a cheap-money policy and the end of the national banks. By the third, they demanded nationalization of the railroads. The cause of the farmers became a moral crusade—they were the victims of those same monopolists against whom Jefferson and Jackson had inveighed. And their present-day defenders (regarding the declining political influence of the farmers as calamitous) reject the fruits of industrialization because, allegedly, America's farmers were its victims. Once again, we are to observe,

11. See J. G. Randall, *The Civil War and Reconstruction* (Boston: D. C. Heath & Co., 1937), *Lincoln the President* (2 vols.; New York: Dodd, Mead & Co., 1945), and *Lincoln the Liberal Statesman* (New York: Dodd, Mead & Co., 1947); A. O. Craven, *The Repressible Conflict* (University, La.: Louisiana State University Press, 1939), and *The Coming of the Civil War* (New York: C. Scribner's Sons, 1942).

an anticapitalist bias not for economic reasons but for political and moral ones.[12]

5. Franklin D. Roosevelt assumed the mantle of Jefferson and Jackson as a leveler and a defender of human rights. That is to say, socially and morally, his identifications were with Jeffersonianism; but not politically. For Roosevelt called upon state interventionism on a grand scale to achieve his intention: the Big State, which Jefferson and Jackson had feared and fought, was his creation. But, because he talked the language of Jefferson, his defenders have turned on the economic ideas of the anti-Roosevelt forces. Capitalism is stagnant and dominated by monopolists; without state intervention the business cycle cannot be resolved, social injustices ameliorated, real wages increased. Once again, the anticapitalism of the New Dealers is political and moral; for certainly no serious case has been made out against capitalism as such.[13]

I should not be misunderstood. I am not condemning the preoccupation of American historians with moral and political ideas. What I am concerned over is the easily accepted assumption that only a leveling interest (in

12. J. C. Ransom *et al.*, *I'll Take My Stand: The South and the Agrarian Tradition. By Twelve Southerners* (New York: Harper & Bros., 1930), and *Who Owns America?* ed. H. Agar and A. Tate, (New York: Houghton Mifflin Co., 1936).

13. See J. N. Frank, *Save America First* (New York: Harper & Bros., 1938).

America more or less to be identified with Jeffersonian-
ism-Jacksonianism-Populism) founds high public policy
on the concept of welfare. The case for conservatism in
America has not been put often enough—in fact, its voice
is very feeble—in moral terms. Burke, Coleridge, Tocque-
ville, and Acton have not their American votaries and
counterparts. Even more seriously, the case for capitalism
lacks impressive defenders. Adam Smith was able to
equate free enterprise with progress; so, interestingly
enough, was Hamilton, who had read Smith closely and
accepted his libertarian as well as his economic ideas.

The case for capitalism in America, as a historical
phenomenon, if properly made, would have many significant lessons for the world today. We must not forget
that its early problems were those of a new and underdeveloped country and that its efforts to create stability
and the basis of an orderly economic progress at home
were linked with the paramount need of establishing
credit-worthiness. In such a history of American capitalism the struggles over central banking, tariffs, public
aid for internal improvements, and an unhampered land
policy play important roles. This is the realm of public
affairs. And in the realm of private enterprise? The will-
ingness and ability to take risks in order to engage in
capital creation (with the failures as well as the successes
recorded) is the heart of the problem. Parenthetically,
it should be pointed out that commercial failure in the
early telegraph, canal, railroad, mining, and automobile

industries in America was enormous. Sound monetary
and credit policy as a public function; risk-taking as a
private one—here in epitome is the history of capitalism.
It is only after such a foundation has been securely laid
that the superstructure of achievement can be erected.
And here I refer to the extraordinary climb of real wages
(without state intervention) in industrialized countries
since the mid-nineteenth century and all those ancillary
benefits in public health and education that can come
only as a result of increases in the national income.

Two asides may be made. If Engels and Marx had
waited another decade—when signs of economic progress
and an impressive rise in real wages were to be observed
on every side—can one assume that *The Condition of
the Working Classes in England in 1844* and the *Communist Manifesto* would ever have been written?

My second passing observation has to do with the
concept of profits. Capitalism has been called the profit
system, and Marx made it synonymous with exploitation.
I submit that economic historians, in part, have been
responsible for the perpetuation of the slander. They have
recorded the individual profits of successful enterprises
without efforts to offset the losses of failure. And they
have been remiss in failing to discuss the faulty accounting of earlier industrial enterprise which, in the case of
individually owned companies, tended to undercapitalize
real worth and in the case of joint-stock companies made
no proper allowances for depreciation and depletion. An

amusing example of undercapitalization was the case of the Carnegie Steel Company, which was capitalized in 1892 at $25,000,000 and in 1900 at $320,000,000. Obviously basing steel profits on the recorded book values of the 1870's and 1880's is silly; for Carnegie purposely held capitalization low in order to keep a whip hand over his working partners. In 1900, when Carnegie was ready to retire from the steel business—and after he had got rid of his troublesome partner H. C. Frick—he permitted a fair valuation of the company's properties to be made.

When, therefore, historians learn to treat their materials more sensitively and make corrections on the counts indicated, the popularly accepted notions about profits as exploitation will undergo drastic revision.

3

The Treatment of Capitalism by
Continental Intellectuals

We view with grave concern the attitude of the Western
intelligentsia to its society. Man possesses mental images,
representations of the universe on progressive scales, of
the things and agents therein, of himself and his relation
to them. These images can be roughly likened to ancient
maps adorned with small figures. Rational action, in
a sense, means to go by the maps available to the ego,
however inaccurate. The breadth, richness, and precision
of these representations or maps are due entirely to inter-
communication. Education consists in conveying a stock
of such images and fostering the natural faculty of producing them. In any group, chosen at random, it can be observed that members are unequally active in communi-
cating such representations; in all organized societies
known to us a fraction of the members is specialized in
dealing with representations. Their importance to society is very great; "rational" individual or collective action must be taken on the basis of what is "known," of
the images of reality which have been given currency.
These images can be misleading. "Rational" action

{ 91 }

based on bad "maps" is absurd in the light of better knowledge and can be harmful; the study of primitive societies yields a quantity of illustrations.

It is rational, subjectively, to tilt at windmills if we firmly believe them to be wicked, dangerous giants holding fair princesses in bondage. It is, however, a sounder view to regard them as a not very efficient device to capture an irregular energy for the purpose of grinding grain. We may happen to dislike the miller, who may be a bad man, but it is, at best, poetic fancy to regard him as blighting the countryside by the spread of his evil wings. The Western intelligentsia is not exempt from such nightmares, resulting from a grafting of strong feeling onto a weak stem of positive knowledge.

Positive knowledge is an understanding of our surroundings which allows us to move toward our goal by the best route. Indeed, some understanding of the forces at work in these surroundings has made it possible to put them to work for our purposes. It is a fact of experience that we can alter the arrangement of men (society) as well as the arrangement of things (nature). As in the former case, this calls for knowledge. To the ignorant, social devices will always appear needlessly complicated; so does a machine. Indeed, any organic structure, as we know, is far more complex than an inorganic one. Men, however, are less willing to admit ignorance in the realm of society than in that of nature:

de re mea agitur. In this social realm, moreover, the criterion of judgment is a dual one.

Men pass judgments of value, some of which are ethical and relate to *bonum honestum;* these latter are never applied to agents or agencies known to be witless. Taken to see a steel furnace, a small child or a savage may be terrified by its roaring and call it "wicked." This view, however, will be dropped as soon as it is understood that the furnace has no spirit. No informed person will think of the furnace as evil because it is fiercely red, lets out occasional streams of burning lava, and feeds on gritty scrap iron and coal that is black. It is merely a device, instrumentally good, since it leads to the production of tools and machines, serving men's purposes. Nor will any reasonable person blame the furnace for the badness of some human purposes served by the machines (such as aggressive war). It is understood that the device is a good servant and that men alone are accountable for evil uses. A schoolboy obdurate in the animist view of the furnace would be shown by his schoolmaster that this is superstition. The same teacher, however, may regard "capitalism" in the same light as the ignorant and superstitious schoolboy regards the furnace. He will see in it an evil monster, author of hurts and wrongs, not a device as useful as the furnace in the production of tools.

It is quite true that moral considerations have their place in the assessing of social devices, while they do not seem germane to the assessing of engineering devices. For in social devices moral agents are involved. Therefore, social devices are subject to a double criterion: efficiency and morality. A discussion of the harmony of these criteria in general involves metaphysics. We shall attempt to remain on a humbler plane. As the notation of good and bad (morally) applies only to consciences, a device can be bad only indirectly. There is a clear case against a device which makes men worse; such is the criterion on which Plato relied to call the politics of Pericles bad. It has been held by some of the greatest minds of mankind that we grow worse through the development of our wants and better by cutting them down. The Stoics pointed out that we become slaves to our desires, and the Cynics stressed that each desire given up is a degree of freedom gained. The early Church Fathers taught that by attention to worldly goods we place ourselves under the sway of the "Prince of this World." More recently Rousseau took up this theme with enthralling eloquence. If this view is adopted, then devices which tend ever to enlarge the scope of our wants by successively satisfying them and by inducing hopes of meeting ever new wants are bad indeed. The social device of capitalism is bad, but so are, by the same token, the engineering devices of industry. This view, however, is not avowed by contemporaries; on the contrary, they are anxious that men's wants should ever increasingly be satisfied. Therefore declamations against "money" do not seem to make sense. If men desire "goods," of course they desire money, which is the common denominator of these "goods," the door opening to them; and the "power of money" is nothing but the *reification* of the power of these goods over men's desires.

It is the proper function of the spiritual and moral teacher to show men the worthlessness of some of the things they do desire. Impeding the acquisition of these things by temporal authority tends to cause lawbreaking and to create a complex of criminal interests. These are among the clearest examples of the deteriorating effect of social devices on human character. The civilized world has marveled at the existence of a powerfully organized criminal society beneath the surface of American life; this mushroom growth was occasioned by the driving-underground of drinking and has been given a new lease on life by the driving-underground of gambling. These phenomena warn us that a result contrary to the intention may be obtained when social devices are used to raise the moral level of human behavior. It is, moreover, well known that any attempt to change man's actions by means other than a change in his spirit is usually futile and anyhow not a moral improvement.

To the intellectual the social device of capitalism offers a displeasing picture. Why? In his own terms, here are self-seeking men in quest of personal aggrandizement. How? By providing consumers with things they want or can be induced to want. The same intellectual, puzzlingly, is not shocked by the workings of hedonist democracy; here also self-seeking men accomplish their aggrandizement by promising to other men things they want or are induced to demand. The difference seems to lie mainly in that the capitalist delivers the goods. And all through the West the fulfilling of political promises seems to be a function of capitalist achievement. Another aspect of the capitalist device which makes it unpleasant to the intellectual is the "degradation of workers to the condition of mere instruments." In Kant's words, it is always immoral to treat other men as means and not as ends. Experience teaches us that this is not an uncommon behavior, nor is it peculiar to capitalism. It is Rousseau's view that such treatment is inherent in civilized society, which multiplies random contacts based on utility rather than on affection, and that it becomes more and more widespread as contacts increase and interests overlap. Marx's view is less philosophical, more dependent on history. The nascent capitalist, he says, found already at hand a population which had been treated as tools by previous exploiters before being seized by the enterprising bourgeois, and the existence of a proletariat which could be treated in such a way originated in the expropriation of the farmers. This is what obliged the workers, bereft of their own means of production, to work for others who disposed of such means. If this theory (obviously inspired by the enclosures) were true, capitalism would have found it most difficult to obtain "wage slaves" in the countries where land was most readily available (i.e., in the United States).

It is not impossible that the mental picture of capitalism has suffered from a dichotomy which classical economists found necessary for logical purposes—the dichotomy of the consumer and the worker. The entrepreneur was represented as serving the consumer and using the worker. Such a dichotomy can be introduced even in the case of Robinson Crusoe, whose physical resources (considered as "the worker") can be represented as exploited in the service of his needs (considered as "the consumer"). This reification of two aspects of the public was intellectually tenable at the outset of what is known as the capitalist era. Heretofore, indeed, the buying public of manufacturers had been sharply distinguished from the working public of artisans, engaged chiefly in producing luxuries consumed by the rich, who lived on unearned takings from the produce of the land. But precisely in the capitalist era the wage-earning producer of industrial consumer goods and the market buyer of such goods have become increasingly identified. It would be a striking illustration of social evolution to find out what fraction of manufactured consumer goods has gone to the wage-earners employed in manufacturing. This fraction has constantly increased under capitalism, so that the dichotomy has become ever a more theoretical concept. It is almost unnecessary to point out that the dichotomy is intellectually useful in any economy where division of labor obtains; in the same manner the Soviet worker is used in the service of the Soviet consumer. The difference lies in the fact that he is used more mercilessly as a worker and gets less as a consumer.

A large part of the Western intelligentsia of today forms and conveys a warped picture of our economic institutions. This is dangerous, since it tends to divert a salutary urge to reform from feasible constructive tasks to the unfeasible and the destructive. The historian's contribution to the distortion of the picture has been under discussion, especially his interpretation of the "Industrial Revolution." I have little to add. Historians have done their obvious duty in describing the miserable social conditions of which they found ample evidence. They have, however, proved exceptionally incautious in their interpretation of the facts. First, they seem to have taken for granted that a sharp increase in the extent of social awareness of and indignation about misery is a true index of increased misery; they seem to have given little thought to the possibility that such an increase might also be a function of new facilities of expression (due partly to a concentration of workers, partly to greater freedom of speech), of a growing philanthropic sensitivity (as evidenced by the fight for penal reforms), and of a new sense of the human power to change things, mooted by the Industrial Revolution itself. Second, they do not seem to have distinguished sufficiently between the sufferings attendant upon any great migration (and there was a migration to the towns) and those inflicted by the factory system. Third, they do not seem to have attached enough importance to the Demographic Revolution. Had they used the comparative method, they might have found that a massive influx into the towns, with the resultant squalor and pauperism, occurred as well in countries untouched by the Industrial Revolution, where they produced waves of beggars instead of underpaid workers. Given population pressure, would conditions have been better without capitalist development? The condition of underdeveloped and overcrowded countries may provide an answer.[1] Methodological oversights of this type, however,

1. Do we not see such countries in dire need of capital for the employment of surplus labor crowded off the land? Be it noted that such labor can be employed on terms which seem to us humane only on condition that its produce serves foreign and richer markets. But, in so far as it destines its wares for the home market, hours have to be long and pay short to make the merchandise salable to a poor population. Indeed, the initial factories seeking to serve an ample fraction of the local population cannot fail to employ their workers on terms much lower than those which were previously commanded by artisans serving only a narrow market of wealthy landowners. Therefore the Industrial Revolution is logically accompanied at the outset by a fall in real wages, if one compares, somewhat unduly, the previous reward of the artisan with the present reward of the factory worker.

dwindle into insignificance in comparison with conceptual errors.

The vast improvement achieved in workers' conditions over the last hundred years is widely attributed to union pressure and good laws correcting an evil system. One may ask, on the other hand, whether this improvement would have occurred but for the achievements of this evil system, and whether political action has not merely shaken from the tree the fruit it had borne. The search for the true cause is not an irrelevant pursuit, since an erroneous attribution of merit may lead to the belief that fruit is produced by shaking trees. Lastly, one may ask whether the "hard times" so bitterly evoked, and for which capitalism is arraigned, were a specific feature of capitalist development or are an aspect of a rapid industrial development (without outside help) to be found as well under another social system. Does the Magnitogorsk of the 1930's compare so favorably with the Manchester of the 1830's?

It is remarkable that the historian should fail to "forgive" the horrors of a process which has played an obvious part in what he calls "progress," precisely in an age addicted to "historicism," where excuses are currently found for horrors going on today on the plea that they will lead to some good, an assertion as yet incapable of proof. Surely indignation is best expended on what is happening today, events which we may hope to influence, rather than on what is beyond recall. Nonetheless, instances readily come to mind of authors who have stressed the hardships of the British working classes in the nineteenth century while finding nothing to say about the violent impressing of Russian peasants into kolkhozes. Here bias is blatant.

Can we find specific reasons for the historian's bias? I think not. The attitude of the historian would present a special problem only if it could be shown that it was he who originally brought to light the evils of capitalism previously unnoticed by the remainder of the intelligentsia, thereby altering the point of view of his fellow-intellectuals. But this is not in accordance with the facts. Unfavorable views of capitalism, whole systems of thought directed against it, were prevalent in large sectors of the intelligentsia before historians exposed the past wrongs of capitalism or indeed before they paid any attention at all to social history. It is probably the main achievement of Marx to have fathered this pursuit, which originated and developed in an anticapitalist climate. The historian is no aimless fact-finder. His attention is drawn to certain problems under the influence of his own or other current preoccupations related to the present day. These induce him to seek certain data, which may have been rejected as negligible by former generations of historians; these he reads, using patterns of thought and value judgments which he shares with at least some contemporary thinkers. The study of the past thus always bears the imprint of present views.

History, the science, moves with the times and is subject to the historical process. Furthermore, there is no philosophy of history but by the application of philosophy to history. To sum up, the historian's attitude reflects an attitude obtaining in the intelligentsia. If he manifests a bias, it is one pertaining to the intelligentsia in general. Therefore it is the intellectual's attitude which must claim our attention.

Sociology and social history are disciplines much favored nowadays. We would turn to them for help. Unfortunately, their scholars have given little or no attention to the problems centering on the intellectual. What is and what has been his place in society? To what tensions does it give rise? What are the specific traits of the intellectual's activity, and what complexes does it tend to create? How have the attitudes of the intellectual to society evolved, and what are the factors in this evolution? All these problems, and many more, should be tempting to social scientists. Their importance has been indicated by major thinkers (such as Pareto, Sorel, Michels, Schumpeter, and, first and foremost, Jean Jacques Rousseau). The infantry of science, so to speak, has not followed; it has left this vast and rewarding field of study uncharted. We must therefore make shift with the scanty data in our possession, and we may perhaps be excused for the clumsiness and blundering of an ill-equipped attempt.

The history of the Western intelligentsia during the

last ten centuries falls easily into three parts. During the first period the intelligentsia is levitic; there are no intellectuals but those called and ordained to the service of God. They are the custodians and interpreters of the Word of God. In the second period we witness the rise of a secular intelligentsia, kings' lawyers being the first to appear; the development of the legal profession is for a long time the main source of secular intellectuals; amusers of noblemen, progressively raising their sights, provide another, very minor, source. This secular intelligentsia grows slowly in numbers but rapidly in influence and conducts a great fight against the clerical intelligentsia, which it gradually supersedes in the main functions of the intelligentsia. Then, in a third period coinciding with the Industrial Revolution, we find a fantastic proliferation of the secular intellectual, favored by the generalization of secular education and the rise of publishing (and eventually broadcasting) to the status of a major industry (an effect of the Industrial Revolution). This secular intelligentsia is by now far and away the most influential, and it is the subject of our study.

An enormous majority of Western intellectuals display and affirm hostility to the economic and social institutions of their society, institutions to which they give the blanket name of capitalism. Questioned as to the grounds of their hostility, they will give *affective* reasons: concern for "the worker" and antipathy for "the capitalist"; and *ethical* reasons: "the ruthlessness and injustice

of the system." This attitude offers a remarkable superficial resemblance to that of the clerical intelligentsia
of the Middle Ages (and a striking contrast, as we
shall see, to that of the secular intelligentsia up to the
eighteenth century). The medieval church centered its
attention and its work on the unfortunate. It was the
protector of the poor, and it performed all the functions
which have now devolved on the welfare state: feeding
the destitute, healing the sick, educating the people.
All these services were free, provided out of the wealth
shunted to them by church taxes and huge gifts, vigor-
ously pressed for. While the church was forever thrusting
the condition of the poor before the eyes of the rich, it
was forever scolding the latter. Nor is its attitude to be
viewed merely in the light of a mellowing of the heart
of the wealthy for their own moral improvement and
the material advantage of the poor. The rich were not
only urged to give but also urged to desist from their
search after wealth. This followed most logically from
the ideal of the Imitation of Christ. The seeking of
worldly goods beyond bare necessity was positively bad:
"Having food and raiment, let us therewith be content.
But they that will be rich fall into temptation and a
snare and into many foolish and hurtful lusts which
drown men in destruction and perdition. For the love of
money is the root of all evil" (I Tim. 6 : 7–10). Obviously of a faith which warned men against worldly goods
("Love not the world, nor the things that are in the

world" [I John 2:15]) could not but regard the most eager and successful seekers after such goods as a vanguard leading the followers to spiritual destruction. The moderns, on the other hand, take a far more favorable view of worldly goods. The increase of wealth seems to them a most excellent thing, and the same logic should therefore lead them to regard the same men as a vanguard leading the followers to material increase.

This latter view would have been most unrealistic in the material conditions of the Middle Ages. In so far as wealth was drawn from land which received no improvements, and in so far as the well endowed did not make productive investments, there was nothing but disadvantage to the many in the existence of the wealthy (though this existence did give rise to the artisan industries from which there long after evolved the industries serving the people; further, it was instrumental in the development of culture). It is perhaps a fact worthy of notice that the modern use of profit, expansion from retained earnings, arose and was systematized in the monasteries; the saintly men who ran them saw nothing wrong in extending their holdings and putting new lands under cultivation, in erecting better buildings, and in employing an ever increasing number of people. They are the true original of the nonconsuming, ascetic type of capitalist. And Berdyaev has truly observed that Christian asceticism played a capital part in the development of capitalism; it is a condition of reinvestment. It is tempting to mention that modern intellectuals look favorably on the accumulation of wealth by bodies of bearing a public seal (nationalized enterprises), which are not without some similarity to monasterial businesses. They do not, however, recognize the same phenomenon when the seal is missing.

The intellectual thinks of himself as the natural ally of the worker. The partnership is conceived, in Europe at least, as a fighting one. The image is imprinted in the intellectual's mind of the long-haired and the blue-bloused standing side by side on the barricades. It appears that this image originated in the French Revolution of 1830 and became generally popular during the Revolution of 1848. The picture was then projected backward into history. A permanent alliance between the thinking few and the toiling many was assumed, a view to which romantic poetry gave expression and currency. The historian, however, can find no evidence of such an alliance in the case of the secular intelligentsia. No doubt the clergy was committed to the solace and care of the poor and unfortunate, and indeed its ranks were continuously replenished from the lowest orders of the people; the clerical intelligentsia was thus the channel whereby the talented poor rose to command princes and kings. But the lay intelligentsia, growing away from its clerical root, seemed to turn its back on the preoccupations of the church. Evidence of its interest in what came in the nineteenth century to be called the "social question" is up to that time remarkably scant. There is, however, abundant evidence of a sustained fight by the lay intellectuals against the welfare institutions of their day, administered by the church. During the Middle Ages the church had amassed immense wealth from pious gifts and foundations for charitable purposes. From the Renaissance to the eighteenth century these accumulations were returned to private possession through far-reaching confiscation. In this process the intellectuals played a major role. Servants of the temporal power, they started from the simple fact that the wealth of the church was least amenable to tax; they moved by degrees to the idea that property was more productive in private hands and hence that private enterprise was the best servant of the prince's treasure. Finally, it became a truism that the prince lost his due and the subject his chance by the piling-up of wealth in undying hands (cf. D'Aguesseau's report on perpetual foundations).[2] The lay intellectuals took little account of the social needs fulfilled by the institutions which they sought to destroy. Beggars should be rounded up and led to forced labor; this was the great remedy, in sharp contrast to the medieval attitude. It is

2. This report, which prefaced the French Royal Edict of August, 1749, lays down the principle that the accumulation of land in collective hands which never release their holdings impedes the availability of capital to the individual, who should find it possible to obtain and control a "fund of wealth" to which he may apply his energy. Readers of this and other state papers will perhaps subscribe to the equation: "The ideas of the French Revolution, I mean those which inspired the ministers of Louis XV."

not an undue comparison to liken the attitude of the secular intelligentsia to that of the most rabid opponents of the social services in our day, except that they went so much further, taking an attitude which we may find recurring in our times a few generations hence, if the social services should happen to claim a large part of the national wealth in a poor economy.

In direct contradiction to the friars who were to live in poverty with the poor, the secular intellectuals started out as companions and servants of the mighty. They can be called friends of the common man in the sense that they fought against distinctions between the high- and the lowborn and that they favored the rising plebeian—in point of fact, the merchant.[3] There was a natural bond of sympathy between the merchant and the civil servant, both waxing important but both still treated as social inferiors. There was a natural resemblance in that both were calculators, weighers, "rational" beings. There was, finally, a natural alliance between the interests of the princes and those of the merchants. The strength of the prince bound up with the wealth of the nation and the wealth of the nation bound up with individual enterprise; these relationships were perceived and expressed as early as the beginning of the fourteenth century by the secular councilors of Philip the Fair of France. The legal servants of the princes tended to free property from its

3. The merchant, of course, was also an industrial promoter, since he ordered from artisans the goods which he offered for sale.

medieval shackles in order to encourage an expansive economy benefiting the public treasury. (All the terms here are anachronistic, but they do not misrepresent the policies of those times.)

Hostility to the money-maker—*l'homme d'argent*—is a recent attitude of the secular intelligentsia. Any history of European literature must cite the names of the numerous money-makers who patronized intellectuals and apparently earned the affection and respect of their protégés; thus the courage shown by the men of letters who defended Fouquet (after the imprisonment of this financier and finance minister by Louis XIV) testifies to the depth of the feelings which he had inspired. The homes of Helvetius and D'Holbach must of necessity figure in any history of the ideas before the French Revolution. These two *hommes d'argent* were much admired by their circle, while the person most popular with French intellectuals at the time of the Revolution was the banker Necker. Again, in the Revolution of 1830, a banker—Laffitte—occupies the front of the stage. But this is the parting of the ways. Later, intellectuals cease to admit the friendship of capitalists, who, in turn, cease to be possible figureheads, as Necker had been.[4]

Strangely enough, the fall from favor of the money-maker coincides with an increase in his social usefulness. The moneyed men whom the French intellectual of the seventeenth and eighteenth centuries had liked so

4. One of the later instances being, of course, that of Engels.

well had been chiefly tax farmers (publicans). The economics of tax farming are simple. The farming companies rented the privilege of collecting a given tax by paying a certain sum to the exchequer. They saw to it that much more than the official levy flowed in to their coffers; the margin constituted their gross income. When the costs of collection had been subtracted, the remainder was clear profit. This procedure is certainly more deserving of the name "exploitation" than any modern form of profit-making. Moreover, these profits were only rarely used for investments enriching the country. The tax farmers were renowned for their ostentatious consumption. As their privilege was valuable, they conciliated influential people at court by "helping them out" very freely. Thus the tax farmer combined all the features commonly attributed to the "bad capitalist" without any of the latter's redeeming features. He produced nothing, he profited in proportion to the harshness of his agents, and he retained his privilege by corruption. What a paradox it is that this type of money-maker should have been popular with the intellectual of his day and that unpopularity should have become the lot of the money-maker at the time when his chief form of money-making became the manufacture of goods for popular use!

Until the late eighteenth century the secular intelligentsia was not numerous; its average intellectual level was therefore high. Moreover, its members were educated in ecclesiastical schools, where they received a strong training in logic, which the "scientific education" of our day seems unable to replace. Therefore these minds were prone to consistency; it is remarkable how common a quality consistent reasoning was in their works, as compared to those of our contemporaries. For minds thus equipped, as soon and in so far as they insulated earthly concerns from spiritual truths, the criterion of earthly good was bound to be what we call efficiency. If, with Descartes, we insulate what occurs in space and comes directly to our notice, we can validly state that one move-ment is greater or less than another and validly call the "force" which causes it greater or less. If social events are regarded as movements, some of which are considered desirable, then it is "good" that these should be pro-duced, the forces which tend to produce them are "good," and devices tending to call them forth and apply them to the object are better or worse in propor-tion to their efficiency. It is a naïve belief of many Euro-pean intellectuals that "efficiency" is an American idol, recently installed. But it is not so. In anything which is regarded *instrumentaliter*, as an agent for the produc-tion of another thing, the greater or lesser capacity of the agent is to be taken into account, and Descartes re-peatedly spoke in this sense of the greater or lesser *vir-tus* of the agent. It seems clear that, the more one tends to a monist conception of the universe which sets up the wealth of society as the result to be attained, the more one must be inclined to equate efficiency in the service of wants and desires with social good. Strangely enough, however, such an evolution of intellectual judgment did not occur in the last hundred and fifty years coincidentally with the evolution toward materialist monism. Ethical judgments disastrously detached from their metaphysical basis sprang up in disorderly growth to plague temporal action.

It seems at least plausible to seek some relation between this change of attitude and the wave of romanticism which swept over the Western intelligentsia. Factory builders trampled over the beauties of nature precisely when these were being discovered; the exodus from the country coincided with a new-found admiration for country life. A sharp change of surroundings divorced men from ancient ways precisely when folkways were coming into fashion. Finally, town life became life with strangers precisely at the moment when civil society was proclaimed insufficient for man's comfort, and the necessity of communal feeling and affection was stressed. All these themes are to be found in Rousseau. This major philosopher was well aware that the values which he cherished were in opposition to the progress of Western society; therefore, he wanted none of this progress: no successive quickening of new wants, no monstrous bellying of towns, no vulgarization of knowledge, etc. He was consistent. Western intellectuals, however, were not to be diverted from their enthusiasm for progress. Therefore, at one and the same time, they thought of industrial development as a great spreading of man's wings and of all its features which were in sharp contrast with the "shepherd" values as deplorable blemishes. Avidity was responsible for these blemishes, no doubt—and also for the whole process! There is a natural homogeneity of the attitudes relative to a certain general process.

The intellectual is really of two minds about the general economic process. On the one side, he takes pride in the achievement of technique and rejoices that men get more of the things which they want. On the other hand, he feels that the conquering army of industry destroys values and that the discipline reigning there is a harsh one. These two views are conveniently reconciled by attributing to the "force" of "progress" everything one likes about the process and to the "force" of "capitalism" everything one dislikes.

It is perhaps worthy of note that precisely the same errors are made in respect to economic creation as are made on the metaphysical level in respect to Creation, since the human mind has but limited capacities and lacks variety even in its mistakes. The attribution to essentially different forces of what is considered good and what is considered bad in the tightly knit process of economic growth of course recalls Manichaeism. Error of this type is not dispelled but tends to be aggravated by retorts taking Pope's line that all is well and that every unpleasant feature is the condition of some good.

It is not surprising that the discussion of the problem

of evil in society should tend to follow the pattern of the more ancient and far-reaching discussion of the problem of evil in the universe, a matter upon which far more intellectual concentration has been brought to bear than upon the more limited modern version. We find the secular intelligentsia passing judgment on temporal organization, not from the point of view of adequacy to the end pursued, but from the point of view of ethics (though the ethical principles invoked are never clearly stated or perhaps even conceived). One hears Western students stating that the welfare of the workers must be the aim of economic leaders; that, although this aim is achieved in the United States and not achieved in the U.S.S.R., it does inspire the Soviet leaders and not the Western leaders (or so the students say); and that therefore the former are to be admired and the latter condemned. Here one finds one's self very clearly in a case of jurisdiction *in temporalia, ratione peccati.* The secular intellectual in this instance does not judge social devices as devices (and the device which achieves the workers' good out of the leaders' indifference *ex hypothesi* is surely an excellent device as compared to that which produces no workers' good out of the leaders' solicitude!), but he steps into the shoes of a spiritual guide, with perhaps insufficient preparation.

Taking a sweeping view of the attitudes successively adopted by the lay intelligentsia of the West, we shall say that it started out in reaction to the spiritual jurisdiction of the clerical intelligentsia, in the services of the temporal powers, and concerned itself with bringing rationality into the organization of earthly pursuits, taken as given. Over the centuries it battered down the power of the church and the authority of revelation; thereby it gave free rein to the temporal powers. Temporal power takes the two basic forms of the sword and the purse. The intelligentsia favored the purse. After liquidating the social power of the church, it turned upon the sword-bearing classes, especially upon the greatest sword-bearer, the political sovereign. The weakening of the ecclesiastical power and of the military power obviously gave full freedom to the moneyed power. But then the intelligentsia turns again, proclaiming a spiritual crusade against the economic leaders of modern society. Is this because the intelligentsia must be at odds with any ruling group? Or are there special causes of antagonism toward business executives?

The intellectual wields authority of a kind, called persuasion. And this seems to him the only good form of authority. It is the only one admitted by intellectuals in their utopias, where the incentives and deterrents of material reward and of punishment are dispensed with. In real societies, however, persuasion alone is inadequate to bring about the orderly co-operation of many agents. It is too much to hope that every participant in an extensive process will play his part because he shares exactly the vision of the promoter or organizer.

This is the hypothesis of the "General Will" applied to every part and parcel of the economic body; it goes to the extremes of unlikeliness. It is necessary that some power less fluctuating than that gained from persuasion should lie in the hands of social leaders; the intellectual, however, dislikes these cruder forms of authority and those who wield them. He sniffs at the mild form of authority given by the massing of capital in the hands of "business czars" and recoils from the rough sort of authority given by the massing of police powers in the hands of totalitarian rulers. Those in command of such means seem to him coarsened by their use, and he suspects them of regarding men as wholly amenable to their use. The intellectual's effort to whittle down the use of alternatives to persuasion is obviously a factor of progress, while it may also, carried too far, lead society into the alternatives of anarchy and tyranny. Indeed, the intellectual has been known to call upon tyranny for the propping-up of his schemes.

The intellectual's hostility to the businessman presents no mystery, as the two have, by function, wholly different standards, so that the businessman's normal conduct appears blameworthy if judged by the criteria valid for the intellectual's conduct. Such judgment might be avoided in a partitioned society, avowedly divided in classes playing different parts and bound to different forms of honor. This, however, is not the case of our society, of which current ideas and the law postulate that it forms a single homogeneous field. Upon this field the businessman and the intellectual move side by side. The businessman offers to the public "goods" defined as anything the public will buy; the intellectual seeks to teach what is "good," and to him some of the goods offered are things of no value which the public should be discouraged from wanting. The world of business is to the intellectual one in which the values are wrong, the motivations low, the rewards misaddressed. A convenient gateway into the intellectual's inner courtyard where his judgments are rendered is afforded by his deficit preference. It has been observed that his sympathy goes to institutions which run at a loss, nationalized industries supported by the treasury, colleges dependent on grants and subsidies, newspapers which never get out of the red. Why is this? Because he knows from personal experience that, whenever he acts as he feels he should, there is unbalance between his effort and its reception: to put it in economic jargon, the market value of the intellectual's output is far below factor input. That is because a really good thing in the intellectual realm is a thing which can be recognized as good by only a few. As the intellectual's role is to make people know for true and good what they did not previously recognize as such, he encounters a formidable sales resistance, and he works at a loss. When his success is easy and instantaneous, he knows it for an almost certain criterion that he has not truly performed his function. Reasoning from his experience, the intellectual suspects whatever yields a margin of profit of having been done, not from belief in and devotion to the thing, but because enough people could be found to desire it to make the venture profitable. You may plead with the intellectual and convince him that most things must be done this way. Still he will feel that those ways are not his. His profit-and-loss philosophy can be summed up in these terms: to him a loss is the natural outcome of devotion to a-thing-to-be-done, while a profit, on the other hand, is the natural outcome of deferring to the public.

The fundamental difference of attitude between the businessman and the intellectual can be pinned down by resort to a hackneyed formula. The businessman must say: "The customer is always right." The intellectual cannot entertain this notion. A bad writer is made by the very maxim which makes him a good businessman: "Give the public what it wants." The businessman operates within a framework of tastes, of value judgments, which the intellectual must ever seek to alter. The supreme activity of the intellectual is that of the missionary offering the Gospel to heathen nations. Selling spirits to them is a less dangerous and more profitable activity. Here the contrast is stark between offering "consumers" what they should have but do not want and offering them what they avidly accept but should not have. The trader who fails to turn to the more salable product is adjudged a fool, but the missionary who would so turn would be adjudged a knave.

Because we intellectuals are functionally teachers of truth, we are prone to take toward the businessman the very same attitude of moral superiority which was that of the Pharisee toward the Publican, and which Jesus condemned. It should be a lesson to us that the poor man lying by the wayside was raised by a merchant (the Samaritan) and not by the intellectual (the Levite). Dare we deny that the immense improvement which has occurred in the condition of the toiling many is chiefly the work of the businessmen?

We may rejoice that we minister to the highest wants of mankind; but let us be honestly fearful of this responsibility. Of the "goods" offered for profit, how many can we call positively harmful? Is it not the case of many more of the ideas we expound? Are there not ideas nefarious to the workings of the mechanisms and institutions which insure the progress and happiness of commonwealths? It is telling that all intellectuals agree to there being such ideas, though not all agree as to which are obnoxious. Far worse, are there not ideas which raise anger in the bosoms of men? Our responsibility is heightened by the fact that the diffusion of possibly mischievous ideas cannot and should not be stopped by the exertion of the temporal authority, while the merchandizing of harmful goods can be so stopped.

It is something of a mystery—and a promising field

of investigation for historians and sociologists—that the intellectual community has waxed harsher in its judgments of the business community precisely while the business community was strikingly bettering the condition of the masses, improving its own working ethics, and growing in civic consciousness. Judged by its social fruits, by its mores, by its spirit, capitalism of today is immeasurably more praiseworthy than in previous days when it was far less bitterly denounced. If the change in the attitude of the intelligentsia is not to be explained by a turn for the worse in what they assess, is it not then to be explained by a change which has occurred in the intelligentsia itself?

This question opens a great realm of inquiry. It has for long been assumed that the great problem of the twentieth century is that of the industrial wage-earner's place in society; insufficient notice has been taken of the rise of a vast intellectual class, whose place in society may prove the greater problem. The intellectuals have been the major agents in the destruction of the ancient structure of Western society, which provides three distinct sets of institutions for the intellectuals, the warriors, and the producers. They have striven to render the social field homogeneous and uniform; the winds of subjective desires blow over it more freely; subjective appreciations are the criterion of all efforts. Quite naturally, this constitution of society puts a premium upon the "goods" which are most desired and brings to the forefront of society those who lead in the production of "goods." The intelligentsia has then lost to this "executive" class the primacy which it enjoyed when it stood as "the First Estate." Its present attitude may be to some degree explained by the inferiority complex it has acquired. Not only has the intelligentsia as a whole fallen to a less exalted status, but, moreover, individual recognition tends to be determined by criteria of subjective appreciation by the public, which the intelligentsia rejects on principle; hence the countervailing tendency to exalt those intellectuals who are for intellectuals only.

We do not presume to explain, and the foregoing remarks are the merest suggestions. Our ambition is merely to stress that there is something to be explained and that it seems timely to undertake a study of the tensions arising between the intelligentsia and society.

PART II

4

The Standard of Life of the Workers in England, 1790–1830

T. S. ASHTON

I

What happened to the standard of life of the British working classes in the late decades of the eighteenth and the early decades of the nineteenth centuries? Was the introduction of the factory system beneficial or harmful in its effect on the workers? These, though related, are distinct questions. For it is possible that employment in factories conduced to an increase of real wages but that the tendency was more than offset by other influences, such as the rapid increase of population, the immigration of Irishmen, the destruction of wealth by long years of warfare, ill-devised tariffs, and misconceived measures for the relief of distress. Both questions have a bearing on some political and economic disputes of our own day, and this makes it difficult to consider them with complete objectivity. An American scholar (so it is said) once produced a book entitled *An Impartial History of the Civil War: From the Southern Point of View.*[1] If I

1. Referred to in Thomas Jones, *Rhymney Memories* (N.p.: Welsh Outlook, 1939), p. 142.

seek to emulate his impartiality, I ought also to strive to equal his candor. Let me confess, therefore, at the start that I am of those who believe that, all in all, conditions of labor were becoming better, at least after 1820, and that the spread of the factory played a not inconsiderable part in the improvement.

There is, it must be admitted, weighty opinion to the contrary. Most of the economists who lived through the period of rapid economic changes took a somewhat gloomy view of the effect of these changes on the workers. "The increasing wealth of the nation," wrote Thomas Malthus in 1798, "has had little or no tendency to better the conditions of the labouring poor. They have not, I believe, a greater command of the necessaries and conveniences of life; and a much greater proportion of them, than at the period of the Revolution, is employed in manufactories and crowded together in close and unwholesome rooms."[2] A couple of generations later J. R. McCulloch declared that "there seems, on the whole, little room for doubting that the factory system operates unfavourably on the bulk of those engaged in it."[3] And, in 1848, John Stuart Mill wrote words that, if they gave some glimmer of hope, were nevertheless highly critical of the society from which the technological changes had

2. Thomas Malthus, *First Essay on Population, 1798* (London: Macmillan & Co., 1926), pp. 312–13.

3. J. R. McCulloch, *Treatises and Essays on Money, Exchange, Interest, the Letting of Land, Absenteeism, the History of Commerce, Manufactures, etc.* (Edinburgh, 1859), pp. 454–55.

sprung. "Hitherto," he said, "it is questionable if all the mechanical inventions yet made have lightened the day's toil of any human being. They have enabled a greater proportion to live the same life of drudgery and imprisonment and an increased number of manufacturers and others to make fortunes. They have increased the comforts of the middle classes. But they have not yet begun to effect those great changes in human destiny, which it is in their nature and in their futurity to accomplish."[4] Alongside the economists was a miscellany of poets, philosophers, and demagogues; parsons, deists, and infidels; conservatives, radicals, and revolutionaries —men differing widely one from another in fundamentals but united in their hatred of factories and in their belief that economic change had led to the degradation of labor.

In the opposing camp there were publicists whose opinions are no less worthy of respect and whose disinterestedness and zeal for reform can hardly be called in question—men like Sir Frederic Eden, John Wesley, George Chalmers, Patrick Colquohoun, John Rickman, and Edwin Chadwick. To offset the passage from Mill, let me quote two sentences from Chadwick, who surely knew as much as anyone else of the squalor and poverty of large numbers of town dwellers in the forties: "The

4. John Stuart Mill, *Principles of Political Economy*, ed. W. J. Ashley (London and New York: Longmans, Green & Co., 1909), p. 751.

fact is, that hitherto, in England, wages, or the means of obtaining the necessaries of life for the whole mass of the labouring community, have advanced, and the comforts within the reach of the labouring classes have increased with the late increase of population. . . . We have evidence of this advance even in many of the manufacturing districts now in a state of severe depression."[5] (He wrote in 1842.)

If a public opinion poll could have been taken, it is probable that the adherents of the first group would have been found to outnumber those of the second. But this is not a matter to be settled by a show of hands. It has been said of the people of Herbert Heaton's native county that they like to speak the truth—especially when it is unpleasant; and there is some evidence that this engaging strait is not found exclusively in Yorkshiremen. Writing to Southey in 1816, Rickman observed, "If one listens to common assertion, everything in grumbling England grows worse and worse";[6] and in a later letter, to a Frenchman, in which he pointed to the way in which the poor had benefited from public relief and cheap food, Rickman was careful to add, "But these arguments would encounter contradiction in England."[7] The romantic re-

5. Edwin Chadwick, *Report on the Sanitary Condition of the Labouring Population of Great Britain* (London, 1843), p. 188.

6. Quoted by M. Dorothy George, *England in Transition* (London: George Routledge & Sons, Ltd., 1931), p. 104.

7. *Ibid.*, p. 137.

vival in literature, which coincided in time with the
Industrial Revolution, tended to strengthen the despon-
dency. Popular writers, like William Cobbett, pictured
an earlier England peopled with merry peasants or sturdy
beef-eating, beer-drinking yeomen, just as their predeces-
sors of the age of Dryden had conjured up the vision of
a Patagonia peopled with noble savages. But neither
native pessimism nor unhistorical romanticism is sufficient in itself to explain the prevalence of the view that
the condition of the workers had deteriorated. It is part
of my thesis that those who held this view had their eyes
on one section of the working classes only.

II

It may be well to begin by making a rapid survey of
the economic and demographic landscape. In these early
decades of the nineteenth century population was increasing rapidly. Whether it is good or ill that more
human beings should experience the happiness and misery, the hopes and anxieties, the ambitions and frustra-
tions of life, may be left for the philosopher or the
theologian to determine. But the increase in numbers was
the result not of a rise of the birth rate but of a fall of
the death rate, and it might be thought that this was
indicative of an improved quality of life. "Human comfort," said Rickman in his letter to Southey, "is to be
estimated by human health, and that by the length of
human life. . . . Since 1780 life has been prolonged by

5 to 4—and the poor form too large a portion of society to be excluded from this general effect; rather they are the main cause of it; for the upper classes had food and cleanliness abundant before."[8] Such an argument was not easy to refute; but Gaskell tried to meet it by declaring roundly that there was no direct connection between mortality and well-being. The noble savage was invoked. In his case, it was asserted, life was "physical enjoyment" and disease "hasty death." For the worker in the manufacturing town, on the other hand, life was "one long disease" and death "the result of physical exhaustion."

If only he had known it, Gaskell might have answered Rickman with a flat denial. For it is now held by statisticians that the fall in the crude death rate was the result of a change in the age distribution of the population and that there was, in fact, no prolongation of the average life. (The deaths per thousand fell simply because population changes in the later eighteenth century had produced a society in which the number of young adults was abnormally high.) But, even if the expectation of life was not raised, it may be urged that the fall of the death rate conduced in some measure to a higher standard of life. For the pomp and circumstances of death and burial swallowed up no small part of the annual income of the workers.[9] When the percentage of deaths to

8. *Ibid.*, pp. 104–5.

9. David Davies, *The Case of Labourers in Husbandry* (Bath, 1795), pp. 23–27.

population fell, the proportion of income devoted to the dead probably diminished and resources were thus freed to add to the comforts of the living.

The growth of population, and, in particular, the increase in the number of people of working age, might well have resulted in a fall of wages. But there took place simultaneously an increase in the supply of other factors of production. Estimates of the national income for this period are few and unreliable. But the statistics of output, expenditure, and consumption all suggest that over the period as a whole it was growing somewhat more rapidly than population. Is there any reason to believe that the proportion of this increased income that went to the workers diminished and that other classes obtained a larger share? This is a question to which no sure answer can be given; all that is possible is to estimate probabilities. In attempting this, it is important to distinguish between the period of the war, the period of deflation and readjustment, and the succeeding period of economic expansion.

During the war heavy government expenditure of an unproductive nature produced a high level of employment but a low standard of comfort. Difficulties of obtaining foodstuffs from abroad led to an extension of the margin of cultivation, and the profit of the farmer and the rent of the landowner increased.[10] Wartime shortages

10. Between 1809 and 1815 rents in the eastern counties and North Wales increased by 40 per cent (R. J. Thompson, "An Inquiry into

of timber, bricks, glass, and other materials limited the construction of houses; high rates of interest and a burdensome property tax reduced the incentives to build. With a growing population and an increased proportion of people of marriageable age the demand for homes increased; urban rents, like agricultural rents, rose. The growth of the national debt led to an expansion of the number of bondholders. The high rates at which loans were floated swelled the income of the passive investor, and, since the tax system was highly regressive, the gain to the rentier was largely at the expense of the poor. Prices in general rose, and, though rates of wages also moved up, they did so more slowly. This, as Earl Hamilton has argued, put additional resources at the disposal of the entrepreneur, and the tendency was reinforced by other, institutional factors.[11] The trader's or manufacturer's token, the "long pay," and the truck system had existed at earlier times. But it is probable that the shortage of coin, which became acute during the period of inflation, led to an extension of these and other devices, the effect of which was to shift purchasing power from the workers to their employers. During the war, then,

---

the Rents of Agricultural Land in England and Wales during the Nineteenth Century," *Journal of the Royal Statistical Society,* LXX [1907], 587–616).

11. Earl Hamilton, "Prices, Wages and the Industrial Revolution," in Wesley C. Mitchell and Others, *Studies in Economics and Industrial Relations* (Philadelphia: University of Pennsylvania Press, 1941).

there took place a whole series of transfers of income—to landlords, farmers, houseowners, bondholders, and entrepreneurs—and these almost certainly worsened the economic status of labor.

The five or six years that followed the peace brought little alleviation. The landlords obtained legislation that enabled them to perpetuate their windfall gains. House rents remained high. Rates of interest fell but slightly.[12] And, though wage rates were less affected than profits, the reduction of government expenditure, the contraction of the currency, banking failures, and a general reluctance to embark on long-term investment reduced the level of activity. Any gains that may have come from the lag of wage rates behind falling prices were probably offset by high unemployment. It is difficult to believe that these years of deflation and civil tumult saw any marked improvement in the condition of the wage-earners.

After 1821, however, economic forces bore less harshly on labor. The gold standard had been restored. A larger quantity of silver and copper was available for the payment of wages. Reforms of the fiscal system were in train. A series of conversions reduced the burden of the national debt, and by 1824 the gilt-edge rate was down to its prewar level of 3.3. Wartime scarcities had disappeared. A more ample supply of bricks and timber combined with cheap money to stimulate the building of factories and

12. The yield on Consols was 4.9 per cent in 1814 and 4.5 in 1815. In 1820 it still stood as high as 4.4.

dwellings. By the early thirties rents (in the north at least) had fallen about 10 per cent, and, in spite of a number of disturbing reports on conditions in the towns, it is fairly clear that the standard of housing was improving. The fall of prices—less marked than in the years immediately after the war—now represented not depression but a reduction of real costs. All in all, the economic climate had become more genial; it was possible for the workers to look forward to better conditions of life and work.

III

So far attention has been directed only to forces internal to the economy. What of those that operated from outside? It has been suggested that over the greater part of this period the power of British exports to exchange for goods from abroad was diminishing and that the unfavorable movement of the net barter terms of trade must have resulted either in lower money incomes for those engaged in the export trades or in higher costs of imported goods. Hence, other things being equal, it must have led to a fall in the standard of life of the workers.

The defects of early British commercial statistics are well known. Since both imports and exports were officially measured by a scale of prices that had become stereotyped in the first half of the eighteenth century, the movements of the figures from year to year represent changes in the volume, and not in the value, of overseas trade.

From 1798, it is true, there are annual figures of the values of exports, derived from the declarations of merchants; but until recently there have been no corresponding estimates of the values of imports for the years before 1854. Mr. Schlote and Mr. Imlah have now filled the gap.[13] I am glad to have this opportunity of paying tribute to the industry and scholarship of Mr. Imlah; every student of the history of international trade must be grateful to him. I have ventured to use his figures to construct crude index numbers of, first, values of British exports; second, the prices of exports and retained imports; and, third, the terms of trade from 1798 to 1836 (see Table 1).[14]

13. Werner Schlote, "Entwicklung und Strukturwandlungen des enlischen Aussenhandels von 1700 bis zur Gegenwart," *Probleme der Weltwirtschaft* (Jena: n.p., 1938), esp. Appendix Table 17. See also Albert H. Imlah, "Real Values in British Foreign Trade," *Journal of Economic History*, VIII (November, 1948), 133–52.

14. The index numbers of prices have been obtained by dividing the index of declared or computed values by that of official values in the case of both exports and imports. The method is open to criticism, for the weighting is curious. The degree of importance assigned to each commodity depends on the rate at which a unit of it was assessed by the inspector general at a time long before that to which the index relates. It depends also on the amount of the commodity imported or exported, and this means that the weighting changes from year to year. My nonmathematical mind is encouraged, however, to believe that this peculiarity does not completely destroy the value of the figures. For Mr. Schlote's index of the terms of trade from 1814 (obtained by dividing a price index of *manufactured* exports by a price index of imports as a whole) is constructed by similar, but more refined, methods, and when adjusted to the same base year it shows, at least until 1832, movements in striking conformity with those of the series offered here.

TABLE 1
EXPORT AND IMPORT PRICES AND THE TERMS OF TRADE
(1829 = 100)

Year	Export Index of Values	Export Price Index	Import Price Index	Net Barter Terms of Trade	Income Terms of Trade
1798	90	264	176	150	51
1799	103	252	183	138	56
1800	105	253	183	138	57
1801	113	255	189	135	60
1802	128	280	150	187	85
1803	103	281	164	171	63
1804	107	262.5	172	153	62
1805	106	255	178	143	60
1806	114	247	164	151	70
1807	104	248	167	148	62
1808	104	237.5	159	149	65
1809	132	220	193	114	68
1810	135	221	188	118	72
1811	92	227	155	146	59
1812	116	220	173	127	67
1813	—	—	—	—	—
1814	127	208	194	107	64
1815	144	187.5	172	109	84
1816	116	183	148	124	78
1817	117	162.5	160	102	73
1818	130	170	178	96	73
1819	98	164	148	111	66
1820	102	148	136	109	75
1821	103	141	120	117.5	86
1822	103	131	119	110	87
1823	99	127	118	108	84
1824	107	123	112	110	96
1825	109	128	137	93	80
1826	88	120	108	111	81
1827	104	111	107	104	97
1828	103	109	103	106	100
1829	100	100	100	100	100
1830	107	98	98	100	109
1831	104	95	102	93	102
1832	102	87.5	96	91	106
1833	111	89	104	85	107
1834	116	87.5	107	82	108
1835	132	94	114	82	116
1836	149	98	120	82	124

From 1803 to 1834 the course of export prices was almost continuously downward. That of import prices was less consistent. From 1802 to 1812 there were wide fluctuations with no marked trend, but from 1814 there

TABLE 2

PRICE RELATIVES OF EXPORTS OF HOME-PRODUCED MANUFACTURES
(1814 = 100)

Year	Cotton Yarn	Cotton Manu-factured	Linen Manu-factured	Woolen Manu-factured	Iron	Total Exports	Total Excluding Cotton Goods
1814	100	100	100	100	100	100	100
1815	83	80	86	101	106	90.6	99
1816	77	77	85	107	98	87.8	95
1817	71	67	79	97	93	78.5	90
1818	74	63	82	99	94	81.9	91
1819	64	70	81	101	92	79.6	88
1820	56	64	77	99	89	71.4	83
1821	49	62	77	87	80	67.6	79
1822	47	57	76	81	71	62.9	76
1823	44	55	71	76	70	60.7	73
1824	42	54	67	73	72	59.3	71
1825	45	54	71	77	90	62.0	78
1826	38	47	65	73	79	57.9	72
1827	36	46	60	65	72	53.6	69

was a descent—steep to 1821, less steep thereafter. The terms of trade moved strongly against Britain during the second phase of the war and less strongly, though markedly, against her from 1816 to the middle thirties. Before jumping, however, to the conclusion that here was a factor pressing heavily on British labor, it may be well to look at the composition of the price index for exports. Table 2 gives the price relatives for some important export commodities for the years 1814–29.[15] It will be observed that the prices of cotton yarn and fabrics fell much more steeply than those of the products of the linen, woolen, and iron industries. During the war manufactured cotton had taken the place of manufactured wool as the British staple export, and during the whole of the first half of the nineteenth century its lead over other commodities lengthened. It was the fall in the price of cotton yarn and cotton cloth that was responsible for the adverse trend of the terms of trade; the prices of exports exclusive of cotton goods actually declined less steeply than those of imports.

The reason for this extraordinary fall is twofold. Instead of producing muslins, cambrics, and other goods of high quality for sale in Europe and the United States, the factories of Lancashire were increasingly concerned with cheap calicoes for Indian and Far Eastern markets; a large part of the fall in price is to be accounted for by a change in the nature of the product of the industry. The other reason was the cost-reducing effect of technical and economic progress. The new mills of the postwar years were driven by steam instead of by water; improvements were being made year after year in the mule and the spinning frame; the power loom was steadily taking the place of the less efficient hand loom; with falling rates

15. The prices have been obtained by dividing the value of the export of each commodity by the quantity exported as recorded by Porter.

of interest capital charges were reduced; and with innovations in transport and trade the expenses of moving and merchanting the goods were diminished. The fall of the prices of cotton yarn and fabrics was not, then, the result of any decline of foreign demand; it reflected a reduction of real costs. And, though the labor cost of a pound of yarn or a yard of calico fell in a spectacular manner, there was no corresponding drop in the earnings of labor. The downward trend of the terms of trade did not represent any worsening of the economic situation either for the nation as a whole or for that part of it that depended on wages.

Figures purporting to show changes in the terms of trade are of dubious value for long-period studies; it is only over short series of years, when the nature of the commodities entering into trade and the state of technique do not change very much, that any safe conclusion can be drawn from them. Even in the short run, indeed, it is far from clear that a downward movement of the index should be taken as a sign of adversity. According to Table 1, the terms of trade moved sharply downward in 1809–10, 1812–15, 1817–18, and 1825—all periods when the volume of trade rose to a peak. They moved sharply upward in 1811, 1816, 1819, and 1826—all years of diminished or stagnant trade. The explanation is, of course, that the prices of British exports rose in times of prosperity and fell in times of depression less violently than those of imports, for the raw materials and foodstuffs Britain imported were inelastic in demand and supply. It would be absurd, however, to suppose that the welfare of the workers diminished when trade was active and increased when trade declined.

An apparatus that is concerned only with prices is clearly inadequate as a measure of changes in the benefits derived from international trade. Not only the cost of living but also the opportunities of earning determine the degree of well-being. Incomes earned by exports provide employment and generate other incomes. How far these incomes will go in the purchase of goods from abroad depends on the prices of imports. In the light of such reasoning a colleague of mine, Mr. Dorrance, recently suggested that a better instrument for measuring the social effects of international trade may be obtained by dividing the indexes of the *values* of exports by those of the *prices* of imports.[16] I have applied his formula to the trade statistics of the period, again making use of Mr. Imlah's figures. The results are shown in the final column of Table 1 under the not altogether satisfactory heading "Income Terms of Trade." Here we have a set of figures free from the paradoxes of those in the preceding column. Both the trend and the year-to-year changes are what our knowledge derived from other sources would lead us to expect. The index shows little change during the war. It rises sharply in 1815 but falls from 1816 to

16. G. S. Dorrance, "The Income Terms of Trade," *Review of Economic Studies,* XVI, No. 39 (1948–49), 50–56.

1819. In these four years of low investment and unemployment forces operating from overseas trade added, it would seem, to the distress. But from 1820 there is a marked upward movement broken only by the slumps of 1825–26 and 1831. In the twenties and thirties incomes derived from overseas trade were increasing, and these incomes purchased more of the goods that came in from abroad. Commerce was exerting an increasingly beneficial influence on the economic life of Britain; and, in view of the fact that the imports consisted largely of such things as tea, coffee, sugar, and the raw materials of industry, it is difficult to believe that the workers had no share in the gain.

IV

It is time to pass from speculation and to say something about such figures as we have relating to wages and the cost of living. The outstanding contribution to our knowledge of the first of these was made forty years ago or more by A. L. Bowley and G. H. Wood. It is based mainly on printed sources, but it is unlikely that further research will invalidate it in any serious way. Nevertheless, it is greatly to be hoped that it may be supplemented by data derived from the wages books which, in spite of bombing and paper salvage, still exist in many scattered factories up and down England. In the hands of careful students these records may be made to yield much information not only about rates of payment but also about actual earnings and sometimes about hours of work and the rents of working-class houses. Until the task is per-formed, it will continue to be impossible to speak with assurance on the topic on which, greatly daring, I have ventured in this paper.

For information about the cost of living we are dependent almost entirely on the work of American scholars. If some of the remarks that follow are critical, I would add that I am filled with shame that English economic historians have done so little in this field and with admiration for the tenacity and skill which American statisticians have brought to the task.

No single contribution to the study of the industrial revolution in England exceeds in importance that made by Norman J. Silberling, whose untimely death has deprived both economic history and statistics of an outstanding exponent. His index number of wholesale prices must remain an indispensable tool for as long ahead as we need look. It is unfortunate that, in my opinion, the same cannot be said of that by-product of his labors, the annual cost-of-living index from 1799 to 1850. This, I need not remind you, is based on the prices of fifteen commodities selected because of their supposed significance to consumers. The prices, however, are chiefly those of the wholesale, not of the retail, market; the index is valid only on the assumption that retail prices moved in the same direction and at approximately the same time as wholesale prices and that the spread between the two remained fairly constant. Now it is true that the structure of retail prices seems to have been far less rigid than it is today. The shopkeeper had not yet fully assumed his function as a shock absorber between merchant and consumer, and the price of a loaf of bread or a pound of beef might double or halve within the course of a few months or even weeks. Several of the commodities used in the index are, however, not consumer's goods at all but merely the raw materials of these. My ancestors of the period did not nourish themselves by munching wheat and oats; they did not cover their nakedness with raw wool and cotton and flax; they were not, literally, shod with leather. According to Silberling, this elementary fact is of small account. "It is well known," he wrote, "in the case of cotton goods that prices adjusted themselves with fair alacrity to the price of raw cotton." When, however, the price relatives of the two are set side by side, we find, as most of us would expect, a considerably greater amplitude of fluctuation in the figures for raw cotton than in those for cotton fabrics. It is surely unrealistic to assume that the prices of food and clothing and footwear are faithfully reflected in those of the substances of which they were made. Also, the prices used by Silberling have been refined by the elimination of customs duties. In actual fact duties constituted a large proportion of the cost of nearly everything brought into the country—a proportion that, moreover (as Mr. Imlah has shown), increased steadily down to the 1840's.

Nor is this all. The man whose scheme of expenditure conformed to that drawn up by Silberling had many idiosyncrasies. He did not occupy a house, or at least he was not called upon to pay rent. He allowed himself only a moderate amount of bread and very little porridge, and he never touched potatoes or strong drink. On the other hand, he got through quite considerable quantities of beef and mutton and showed a fondness for butter. Perhaps he was a diabetic. The ordinary Englishman of the eighteenth century would have been puzzled by him. For this ordinary Englishman (like his descendant of 1949) was a granivorous and not a carnivorous animal. His staple of diet was bread or, in the north of England, oatmeal; meat was for him a luxury to be taken once, or at most twice, in the week. Silberling's creature who quenched his thirst only with tea and coffee (with sugar but without milk) would have seemed to him a poor sort of fish. For however abstemious the ordinary Englishman may have been in respect to meat and many other things, he took small beer with each main meal of the working day and ale, in no small measure, whenever he had occasion to celebrate.

The portrait that appears in the scholarly pages of Elizabeth Gilboy has somewhat different features.[17] In

17. Elizabeth W. Gilboy, "The Cost of Living and Real Wages in Eighteenth Century England," *Review of Economic Statistics*, XVIII (1936), 134–43.

her index, cereals have a weight of 50 per cent of the
total, as against 32 per cent assigned to them by Silberling, and animal products are rightly given a lower
status. But her prices are those that were paid by hos-
pitals, schools, and government departments and not by
individual workmen; they are contract and not truly retail prices. Moreover, they are mainly London prices.
One of the outstanding features of English life was (and
still is) its regional variety. The prices of foodstuffs
varied greatly between one part of the country and
another, and it was not uncommon for something approaching a local famine to coincide with conditions of
relative abundance at places only a hundred miles or so
away. As improvements were made in transport by river,
road, and canal, prices in the provinces tended to come
into line with those of the metropolis. "All the sensible
people," wrote Arthur Young in 1769, "attributed the
dearness of their country to the turnpike roads; and reason speaks the truth of their opinion . . . make but a
turnpike road through their country and all the cheap-
ness vanishes at once." But even fifty or more years later
there were many areas of England without turnpikes. In
these areas the prices of foodstuffs might be either lower
or higher than in London; they were certainly subject to
wider fluctuations.

No one has done more than Mrs. Gilboy to make us
aware of local variations in the price of labor. But she has

not taken full account of the possibility of a similar variation of retail prices or of local peculiarities of diet. Oatmeal remained the staple food of the poor in the north,
and rye bread the staple in the Midlands, long after
wheaten bread had come into common use in London
and the south. To apply contract prices derived from
the metropolitan area, and a system of weights based on
metropolitan habits, to the earnings of workers in the
provinces is indeed a hazardous procedure. What some-
one has unkindly called Mrs. Gilboy's bricklayers dressed
up as bluecoat boys[18] would hardly have been recognized
as brothers by the pitmen of Northumberland or the
weavers of Lancashire or Somerset.

But, if the scheme of expenditure varied from place
to place, it varied also from time to time. Rufus T. Tucker,
whose gallant attempt to trace the course of real wages
of London artisans over two centuries must excite admiration, shows himself alive to this difficulty. His solution
is to abandon the use of a fixed yardstick. When some
new commodity seems to become significant in the
workers' budget, a place is found for it, and the weights
attached to other things are adjusted. Mr. Tucker divided
the figures in his index of wages (for our period the
wages of four kinds of building labor at Greenwich and
Chelsea) by his chain index of prices in order to determine "the ability of a typical, regularly employed Lon-

18. Boys attending a charity school, at which they wear long blue
coats or gowns.

don artisan to purchase commodities of the sort artisans customarily purchased."

This typical London artisan was no static figure. At first his consumption was limited to a few commodities, including some inferior grain stuffs. Later he spread his expenditure over a wider range of goods, some of which were relatively expensive ("the commodities of the sort artisans customarily purchased" had changed). One might have supposed that the wider choice now open to him was one element in a rising standard of living. But no. Mr. Colin Clark has used Tucker's figures to support his thesis that average real income fell "from a fairly high level in the seventeenth century to an Asiatic standard at the beginning of the nineteenth." That Asiatic standard, I may remark in passing, included tea and sugar and some other minor products of Asia hardly known to the London artisan of the seventeenth century. Would the man of the early nineteenth century really have welcomed a return to the diet of his great-great-grandfather? The reception he gave to some well-intentioned efforts to induce him to use rye instead of wheat in his bread hardly leaves one in doubt regarding the answer. Like the laborers of Nottinghamshire, he replied that he had lost his "rye teeth."[19]

Mr. Tucker's artisan was peculiar in another respect.

19. See C. R. Fay, *The Corn Laws and Social England* (Cambridge: Cambridge University Press, 1932), p. 4.

Whatever his income, he always spent one-sixth of it on rent or one-fifth on rent and services combined. This is a proportion far higher than any I have been able to discover in other areas, but, no doubt, dwellings were dear in London. It is the fixity of habit that is peculiar. Mr. Tucker says that his index "attempts to measure the workman's ability to purchase housing." But, if it is true that the workman always spent a fixed proportion of his income on housing, would not the figures of wages alone serve as a measure of that ability? In fact, rents are perhaps the most difficult of all prices to draw into an index number. Few consumer goods are completely standardized. A loaf of bread at a given time and place may be a very different commodity from a loaf at another time and place. "The veal that is sold so cheap in some distant counties at present," wrote Malthus, "bears little other resemblance than the name, to that which is bought in London."[20] But this variation of quality is especially marked in the case of houses. A cottage with a living room and a single bedroom is a different commodity from one with four rooms and an attached washhouse or loom shed. A cottage near a factory would usually produce a higher rent than one far distant; for the tenant of the first not only avoided a long walk to and from work but was also able, if he wished, to increase his

20. *Op. cit.*, p. 317.

income by working overtime without trenching unduly on the hours of sleep.[21]

The truth is that it is not possible to compare the welfare of two groups of people separated widely in time and space. We cannot compare the satisfaction derived from a diet that includes bread, potatoes, tea, sugar, and meat with that derived from a diet consisting mainly of oatmeal, milk, cheese, and beer. In the early and middle decades of the eighteenth century only a narrow range of commodities competed for the surplus income of the workers. That is why (to the distress of the well-to-do observer) any easement of the position of the poor was taken out in the form of more drink and more leisure— or in "debauchery and idleness," as the sedate and leisured observer usually put it. Later in the century the range of commodities available widened, and after the French wars new opportunities of travel and education were opened up. No index number can possibly take full account of such matters.

I have made these criticisms and asked these questions in no carping spirit. My object is simply to point to the difficulties of measuring arithmetically changes in the standard of living. The pioneers, as so often happens, have attempted too much. We must restrict our ambitions, realize the limitations of our bag of tricks, and refrain

21. A point made in an unpublished thesis by Walter Lazenby, "The Social and Industrial History of Styal, 1750–1850" (University of Manchester, 1949).

from generalizations. We cannot measure changes in real wages by means of an index of wholesale or institutional prices. We cannot apply the price data of one area to the wage data of another. We cannot safely draw up a table to cover a long series of years during the course of which changes may have occurred not only in the nature and variety of the goods consumed but also in human needs and human wants. We require not a single index but many, each derived from retail prices, each confined to a short run of years, each relating to a single area, perhaps evn to a single social or occupational group within an area.[22]

I cannot hope at this stage to meet these requirements. All I have to offer are three short tables exhibiting the changes in the cost of staple articles of diet in the area that is often spoken of as the cradle of the factory system. Such virtue as they possess derives from the fact that they are based on retail prices recorded by contemporaries. The first relates to Oldham, a textile town five or six miles from Manchester. The figures are drawn from an unpublished manuscript entitled "The Chronol-

22. This is a view taken by a distinguished statistician. "I do not belief that index numbers can serve over very long periods. If the same form is used throughout the difficulty of shifts in the 'preference map' cannot be overcome. If the index is obtained by drawing together different forms, then a bias is to be expected, a bias which tends to be amplified over time: In general, index numbers are to be limited to short-run comparisons" (R. G. D. Allen, "The Economic Theory of Index Numbers," *Economica*, XVI [N.S.], No. 63 [August, 1949], 197–203).

ogy or Annals of Oldham" by William Rowbottom,[23] and I am greatly indebted to a former colleague, Miss Frances Collier of the University of Manchester, for the toil involved in extracting them. Like other annalists of

TABLE 3

INDEX OF COST OF DIET IN OLDHAM

(1791 = 100)

Year	Oat-meal	Flour	Pota-toes	Beef	Mut-ton	Ba-con	But-ter	Cheese	Total Cost of Diet
1791 Spring	100	100	100	100	100	100	100	100	100
1792 Spring	105	90	85	100	100	100	100	60	94
1793 Fall	126	102	154	80	100	100	106	90	113
1794	—	—	—	—	—	—	—	—	—
1795 January	121	110	154	110	110	94	112	100	117
1795 May–June	132	151	185	120	120	106	112	110	138
1796	—	—	—	—	—	—	—	—	—
1797	84	82	100	130	130	106	112	130	98
1798	—	—	—	—	—	—	—	—	—
1799 Spring	103	73	85	100	100	88	112	110	92
1800 May	316	245	309	180	180	131	175	200	249
1801 January	290	270	309	160	160	150	188	180	253
1801 October	112	122	92	160	170	150	125	140	124
1802 January	126	135	92	176	180	138	115	132	133
1803 January	100	116	123	160	160	138	138	132	123
1804 January	142	114	154	160	160	124	162	154	139
1805	—	—	—	—	—	—	—	—	—
1806 January	153	141	115	140	140	100	144	154	139
1807 January	—	—	—	—	—	—	—	—	—
1808 January	153	133	185	140	140	112	175	140	148
1809 January	163	176	123	154	154	112	175	170	158

the period, Rowbottom began by describing the more sensational events, such as murders and thefts, which occurred in the locality. For 1787 and the succeeding three years there is little of economic interest in his manuscript. But in 1791 he began to make jottings about

23. Transcript by Giles Shaw now in the Manchester Public Reference Library.

the prices charged by shopkeepers in Oldham, and as time went on the range of his observations widened and the record became more systematic. There are many months and some years for which little or no information about prices is given; and there are several commodities, such as sugar, treacle, malt, coal, and candles, the prices of which are given so infrequently as to make it impossible to include them in the index.

When Rowbottom began to keep his record, most of his fellow-townsmen were still domestic workers employed in weaving fustians, calicoes, and checks or making hats. Their staple diet consisted of bread, oatmeal porridge, potatoes, and a little beef and mutton. In compiling the index, I have accordingly given a weight of 4 each to oatmeal and flour, 2 to potatoes, and 1 each to beef, mutton, bacon, butter, and cheese. It will be noticed that the prices of the first three of these fluctuated more violently than those of the others. The very poor, who lived chiefly on meal and potatoes, suffered much in 1795 and were reduced to extremities in 1800–1801. In these two years of famine, Rowbottom records, new kinds of cereals, such as barley flour and "American flour" (presumably of corn), were on sale. The poor gathered docks, "green sauce," and water cresses to serve as a substitute for potatoes, and nettles were on sale in Oldham at twopence a pound.

The same picture of wide fluctuations in the cost of a standard diet is shown in the figures for the years 1810–

T. S. Ashton

19 (see Table 4). These are drawn from a table giving details of wages, the price of provisions, and expenditure on poor relief published in the *Manchester Mercury* of January 18, 1820. They relate to "Manchester and the other principal seats of the Cotton Manufacture," and, although the source is not disclosed, the prices are said

TABLE 4

INDEX OF COST OF DIET IN MANCHESTER AND OTHER TEXTILE TOWNS
(1810 = 100)

Year	Oatmeal	Flour	Pota-toes	Beef Best	Beef Coarse	Bacon	Butter	Cheese	Index of Cost of Diet
1810	100	100	100	100	100	100	100	100	100
1811	100	91	100	100	100	82	112	100	97
1812	150	127	165	100	100	91	108	100	129
1813	130	111	120	106	108	100	119	106	116
1814	93	76	110	112	117	100	119	100	96
1815	87	69	110	100	108	95	112	100	91
1816	83	80	110	94	92	73	85	79	86
1817	127	120	130	94	92	64	85	79	111
1818	107	91	135	100	100	91	108	94	97
1819	90	73	130	100	100	91	92	94	86

to be "the average retail prices of each year, according to the best information that could be procured." Again it is clear that the prices of grain foods and potatoes were more volatile than those of meat, bacon, butter, and cheese. The table suggests that the cost of the standard diet fell little, if at all, in the four years of depression and distress that followed the end of the war.

The figures in Table 5 relate to Manchester. They are taken from an estimate of the retail cost of provisions made by the Manchester Chamber of Commerce and published in an appendix to *Manchester Merchants and Foreign Trade* by Arthur Redford.[24] They indicate that throughout the twenties the cost of the staple diet moved to a higher rather than to a lower level.

I have resisted the temptation to throw these three

TABLE 5

INDEX OF COST OF DIET IN MANCHESTER
(1821 = 100)

Year	Oatmeal	Flour	Pota-toes	Beef Best	Beef Coarse	Pork	Bacon	Cheese	Index of Cost of Diet
1821	100	100	100	100	100	100	100	100	100
1822	94	117	79	100	117	96	115	95	102
1823	100	92	88	100	108	135	112	121	101
1824	116	115	141	115	117	139	127	126	122
1825	116	119	106	125	158	135	138	137	120
1826	122	112	172	125	158	130	115	137	130
1827	128	112	84	120	133	139	115	147	119
1828	119	119	100	130	133	130	123	132	120
1829	106	127	115	120	125	130	100	132	118
1830	112	119	106	110	100	113	115	105	112
1831	112	115	110	120	117	122	123	116	115

figures together so as to offer a single index of the cost of provisions from 1791 to 1831, partly because of slight differences of area and of the range of commodities but mainly because the data are not derived from a common source. The outlines are, however, clear. Following a fall after the famine of 1800–1801, the upward movement of prices continued, to a peak in 1812. Thereafter food prices fell to about 1820 but rose again during the following decade. In 1831 the standard diet of the poor

24. Manchester: Manchester University Press, 1934.

can hardly have cost much less than in 1791.[25] If this was so, it would seem that any improvement in the standard of living must have come either from a rise in money wages or from a fall in the prices of things not included in this index. One of the striking features of domestic production was the wide variations in the prices offered for labor. In December, 1793, according to Rowbottom, the weavers of ginghams at Oldham received 10s. per end; in April, 1794, they were paid 19s. and in August of the same year 24s. 4d. During the same period the price of weaving nankeens rose from 16s. to 26s. a piece. Generally, for reasons set forth by Adam Smith, the price of labor rose when the cost of provisions fell and years of dearth were usually years of low wages. In these circumstances the standard of life of the worker was subject to violent fluctuation. One of the merits of the factory system was that it offered, and required, regularity of employment and hence greater stability of

25. The first of each of the following figures is the price at Oldham in 1791, the second that at Manchester in 1831: meal (per peck) 19d., 18d.; flour (per peck) 24d., 30d.; potatoes (per load) 6s. 6d., 6s. 3d.; beef (per pound) 5d., 6d.; pork (per pound) 5d., 5½d.; bacon (per pound) 8d., 7d.; cheese (per pound) 5d., 8d. The cost of diet in 1810 was apparently about 5 per cent higher than in 1809 and 60 per cent higher than in 1791. For purposes of comparison with the figures in Table 3 the figures in Table 4 should be increased by 60 per cent.

Between 1819 and 1821 there was a marked drop in the prices of most of the commodities in the index. Roughly the cost of diet in 1821 was the same as in 1791, and the figures in Table 5 are broadly on the same base as those in Table 3. The sample basket of commodities cost about 15 per cent more in 1831 than in 1791.

consumption. During the period 1790–1830 factory production increased rapidly. A greater proportion of the
people came to benefit from it both as producers and as
consumers. The fall in the price of textiles reduced the
price of clothing. Government contracts for uniforms and
army boots called into being new industries, and after
the war the products of these found a market among the
better-paid artisans. Boots began to take the place of
clogs, and hats replaced shawls, at least for wear on
Sundays. Miscellaneous commodities, ranging from clocks
to pocket handkerchiefs, began to enter into the scheme
of expenditure, and after 1820 such things as tea and
coffee and sugar fell in price substantially. The growth
of trade-unions, friendly societies, savings banks, popular
newspapers and pamphlets, schools, and nonconformist
chapels—all give evidence of the existence of a large
class raised well above the level of mere subsistence.[26]

26. In 1837 or 1838 Thomas Holmes, an old man of eighty-seven,
born in 1760, gave to a member of the Liverpool Statistical Society
his impressions of the changes that had taken place since his youth
at Aldbrough (Holderness) : "There has been a very great increase
in the consumption of meat, wheaten bread, poultry, tea and sugar.
But it has not reached the poorest, except tea, sugar, and wheaten
bread. The poorest are not so well fed. But they are better clothed,
lodged and provided with furniture, better taken care of in sickness
and misfortune. So they are gainers. This, I think, is a plain statement of the whole case."

Referring to mechanics and artificers, he says, "The wages of almost all have increased in a proportion faster than the rise in the
expenses of living." When asked, "Are the poorer classes more intelligent?" he replied, "Beyond all comparison."

There were, however, masses of unskilled or poorly skilled workers—seasonally employed agricultural workers and hand-loom weavers in particular—whose incomes were almost wholly absorbed in paying for the bare necessaries of life, the prices of which, as we have seen, remained high. My guess would be that the number of those who were able to share in the benefits of economic progress was larger than the number of those who were shut out from these benefits and that it was steadily growing. But the existence of two groups within the working class needs to be recognized. Perhaps the explanation of the division of opinion, to which I called attention at the beginning of this paper, rests on this. John Stuart Mill and his fellow-economists were thinking of the one group; Rickman and Chadwick had their eyes fixed on the other.

5

The Factory System of the Early Nineteenth Century

W. H. HUTT

The early British factory system may be said to have been the most obvious feature of the Industrial Revolution. Forecasting as it did the trend of subsequent industrial development, judgments passed upon it will largely determine the attitude taken with regard to the modern industrial system.

There is reason to believe that the form that factory development abroad assumed was due, in no small degree, to imitation, direct or indirect, in Great Britain, and factory legislation the world over was framed on the British model. There are still parts of the world where industrial conditions seem to resemble those which existed here a century ago, and a recent article on conditions in China reads, in parts, exactly like a quotation from one of the history books which describe the early English system.[1] One suspects that the similarity is partly due to the author having read these modern history books, but a more or less parallel situation undoubtedly exists.

1. "Labour Conditions in China," *International Labour Review*, December, 1924.

W. H. Hutt

In the course of another line of inquiry, the writer of this essay was led to study a selection of the voluminous parliamentary reports and other literature of the early nineteenth century bearing on labor conditions. He was struck with the fact that the impressions he obtained from these publications were very different from those which certain modern works on the early factory system had given him, namely, *A History of Factory Legislation* by Hutchins and Harrison and *The Town Labourer* and *Lord Shaftesbury* by J. L. and Barbara Hammond. As these works are practically the standard modern works, he felt that a critical examination of the main evidence and more important discussions of the subject was necessary. This essay is the result of an attempt at such an examination.

Perhaps an explanation of the point of view of the authorities just referred to can be found in the weight they attach to the evidence given before what has come to be known as "Sadler's Committee," in 1832.[2] The report of this committee gives us a dreary picture of cruelty, misery, disease, and deformity among the factory children, and this picture is generally accepted as authentic. The Hammonds refer to the report as "a classical document." They continue: "It is one of the main sources of our knowledge of the conditions of factory life at the time. Its pages bring before the reader in the

2. *Report of Select Committee on Factory Children's Labour, 1831–32.*

vivid form of dialogue the kind of life that was led by the victims of the new system."[3] Hutchins and Harrison regard it as "one of the most valuable collections of evidence on industrial conditions that we possess."[4]

What do we know of this committee? Sadler was making desperate efforts to get his "Ten Hours' Bill" through Parliament. When it came up for second reading, the House decided that a committee should be set up to investigate the story of gross brutalities in the factories, which he had described at great length and with much eloquence. Sadler himself presided, and it was agreed, for reasons of economy and convenience, that he should call his witnesses first, after which the opponents of the bill should put their case. He exercised the greatest energy to get his case complete by the end of the session, and then, ignoring the demands of justice, he immediately published the evidence "and gave to the world such a mass of *ex-parte* statements, and of gross falsehoods and calumnies . . . as probably never before found their way into any public document."[5] The question had, in fact, become a party question, and a balanced discussion was impossible.[6]

3. J. L. and Barbara Hammond, *Lord Shaftesbury* (London: Constable, 1923), p. 16.

4. B. L. Hutchins and A. Harrison, *A History of Factory Legislation* (London, 1903), p. 34.

5. R. H. Greg, *The Factory Question* (London: A. Cobbett, 1837).

6. See speech of Wilson Patten in House of Commons (Hansard, XVII, 79 [1833]).

To say that the report is one-sided as regards the evidence contained in it would be a mild criticism. It consists chiefly of individual and carefully selected instances. Moreover, Sadler had made use of an effective propagandist device in calling evidence of what happened in earlier times and presenting it in such a way as to suggest that the same abuses were still in operation.[7] This was particularly unfair, as the previous thirty years had been accompanied by considerable material improvements and advances, both within and outside the factories, and these changes had been followed by adjustments in social standards. A serious defect in the evidence is that *it was not given on oath.* If we take into account the religious feeling of the day, the importance of this must be clear. Of the three witnesses who came from Manchester,[8] only one could be got to repeat his evidence before the subsequent commission, and then he would not do so on oath. His evidence was found by the commission to be "absolutely false."

7. Fielden made use of the same device in *The Curse of the Factory System* (1836). It is improbable, even in the early days of the factory system, when work-house apprentices made up the greater part of child labor, that the picture of horror which Sadler and Fielden drew could have been in the least typical. Even Robert Owen admitted that, when he purchased his mill in 1799, the apprentice children were "well fed and clothed and lodged, and, to a superficial observer, healthy in their countenances" (*Report of Select Committee on the State of the Children Employed in the Manufactories of the United Kingdom* [1816] ["Peel's Committee"]).

8. And there were only three called, although the inquiry practically resolved itself into one on cotton factories!

These are not merely charges made by interested manufacturers. The unsatisfactory nature of Sadler's *Report* was freely admitted by most of the earlier opponents of the factory system who had not become involved in party politics. Even Engels, Karl Marx's comrade-in-chief, describes the *Report* thus: "Its report was emphatically partisan, composed by strong enemies of the factory system for party ends. . . . Sadler permitted himself to be betrayed by his noble enthusiasm into the most distorted and erroneous statements."[9] Another, though more sober, opponent of the factory system describes the position thus: "The whole affair assumed at this time the character of a political party qustion, the Tories for the greater part still smarting under their defeat on the reform question, and endeavouring with delight to bring to the surface everything likely to damage, in the eyes of the public, the industrial middle class."[10]

Can we wonder that the manufacturers were furious at Sadler's maneuver and at their demand for a further inquiry? All Hutchins and Harrison tell us about this is that, although the manufacturers' interests "had been well represented upon it [Sadler's Committee], they were discontented with the results, and now pressed for a fur-

9. Friedrich Engels, *Condition of the Working Classes in 1844* (London, 1892), p. 170.

10. E. von Plener, *English Factory Legislation* (London, 1873), p. 10.

ther enquiry on the spot."[11] Dr. Slater says that the manufacturers' anger was "at the unusual action of the Committee in taking evidence from the sufferers themselves."[12] Why this consistent unfairness to the manufacturers?

In the reports issued by the subsequent commission[13] we can find effective answers to nearly all the charges made before the committee, but few writers mention this; for the most part they proceed as though the stories brought before the committee were confirmed.[14] We can judge of the difference in the character of the evidence by noticing that R. H. Greg, a fierce critic of Sadler's Committee, could nevertheless refer to the evidence published by the Factory Commission as "an official and authenticated mass of evidence to which all must bow." In particular, the charge of systematic cruelties to chil-

11. Hutchins and Harrison, *op. cit.*, p. 35.

12. Gilbert Slater, *The Making of Modern England* (London: Constable, 1913), p. 122.

13. *First and Second Reports of the Commission on the Employment of Children in Factories* (1833) and the *Supplementary Report* (1834).

14. Wing did argue definitely that these reports abundantly confirmed the evidence given before Sadler's Committee (*Evils of the Factory System* [London, 1837], p. xix). H. de B. Gibbins devotes three pages of his *Industry in England* to a discussion of the evidence given before this committee but says nothing about the commission which followed. His account of the factory system seems to have been based almost entirely upon an uncritical acceptance of the violently partisan writings of Whately Cooke Taylor and Samuel Kydd.

dren was shown to have been entirely without foundation, and we do not think that any careful student reading these reports could doubt that such deliberate cruelties as did exist were practiced on the children by the operatives themselves, against the will and against the knowledge of the masters. The masters were, on the whole, as many of their opponents admitted, "men of humanity."

In spite of the mass of material which we have, it is difficult for us to obtain a clear picture of the physical and moral condition of the factory children. A good deal, perhaps the most valuable part, of our information comes from the evidence of medical men, but neither the Hammonds nor Hutchins and Harrison make any attempt to *assess* the value of their evidence. It is not an easy thing to do, even when we believe the doctors to have been free from a particular bias. There are two main difficulties. First, the state of mind of many of those who set out to observe the state of health of a particular group of people suggests *le malade imaginaire;* second, the condition of medical knowledge was such that medical *opinions* (as opposed to *observations*) are valueless. "Bleeding" was still the favorite remedy for most complaints.[15] The doctors were, however, at least deliberate observers, and, while their *experiences* are illuminating, their *abstract theories* do not help us at all. One would

15. There were speculations among some doctors as to the purifying qualities of smoke, gas, emanations, etc. (Philip Gaskell, *The Manufacturing Population of England* [London, 1833], p. 265).

almost think that the Hammonds and Hutchins and Harrison hold the reverse. They both accept the medical evidence given before Peel's Committee in 1816,[16] which was favorable to the reformers' case, but reject as biased that given before the Lords' Committee[17] two years later, which was favorable to the manufacturers' case.

Let us compare the medical evidence contained in the reports of these two committees. The nine doctors called before Peel's Committee gave practically nothing but a mass of abstract opinions. Six of them confessed to knowing nothing whatever of "manufactories" except by hearsay; one had known a factory "as a very young man"; one confessed to being a personal friend of Nathaniel Gould; and the other (Kinder Wood), although a friendly witness, largely contradicted the evidence of the rest. They were questiond in the following style: "Supposing that children at an early age . . .?" They replied by giving their opinion as to what would happen (or should happen) under those conditions, never having actually observed children under those circumstances.

Now let us consider the Lords' Committee of 1818. The Hammonds seek to discredit it by observing that it "discovered doctors of standing ready to swear that factory life was most wholesome for children, and that it was doubtful whether it would hurt them to work

16. *Op. cit.*

17. See Lords' Sessional Papers, 1818, Vol. IX.

twenty-three hours out of the twenty-four."[18] They add nothing to this, so we must take it as intended to convey their impression. Hutchins and Harrison say: "Some of the medical evidence before the Lords' Committee suggests that at least one or two of the doctors summoned were literally suborned by the masters, so extraordinary were their shifts and evasions to escape answering the questions put to them."[19] There is little to justify either of these observations. The doctors called *had*, in this case, practical experience of "manufactories" and had *observed* children employed in them, and their evidence, generally, suggested that, whatever the hours factory children were actually working at that period, they were at least as healthy as children not employed in factories. The only "shifts and evasions" that we find were merely attempts, under severe cross-examination by Sarjeant Pell, who had been briefed for the purpose, to avoid expressing abstract opinions not based upon actual observation. One doctor (E. Hulme) was asked: "You, as a medical man, then, can form no opinion, independent of evidence, as to the number of hours that a child might, or might not be employed, that would or would not be injurious to his health?" The answer was, "I can't." Is this a shifty or evasive reply? Again and again before

18. Hammond and Hammond, *Lord Shaftesbury*, p. 11; see also *The Town Labourer* (London and New York: Longmans, Green & Co., 1917), p. 167.

19. *Op. cit.*, p. 26.

this committee we come across the declaration that a speculative opinion, or one founded on abstrcat grounds only, as to the number of hours a child could work without harm was impossible. To illustrate the futility of attempting to determine a theoretical limit by mere speculation, Hulme replied as follows: "If there were such an extravagant thing to take place, and it should appear that the person was not injured by having stood twenty-three hours, I should then say it was not inconsistent with the health of the person so employed." A comparison of this passage with the Hammonds' description of the incident, quoted above, may help us to appreciate their scientific attitude.[20] As Hulme explained: "My answer only went to this effect, that it was not in my power to assign any limit."[21]

The most interesting contribution from the medical antagonists of the factory system came from Dr. Turner Thackrah, under the title of *The Effects of the Principle Arts, Trades and Professions on Health and Longevity* (1831). This book became almost a bible to Oastler and Sadler and was copiously quoted by a long succession of reformers. Yet it was in no sense a partisan work, and its author had not been drawn into any party political movement. The Tory press of London must have felt very undecided as to how to take him, for he reminded the

20. Perhaps they have relied upon the mangled version in Whately Cooke Taylor's *Modern Factory System* (London, 1891).

21. Lord's Sessional Papers, 1818, IX, 22.

editors that, while they were supporting Sadler in his "Ten Hours'" agitation, their own staffs were worked, "I am told, fifteen to seventeen hours a day!"[22] Thackrah set out to examine scientifically and to compare the health of people engaged in all the principal occupations of the day, and it was only by partial quotation that the reformers were able to make such a wide use of his work. Certainly he opposed child labor with considerable warmth (whether inside or outside the factories) on the ground that "the term of physical growth ought not to be a term of physical exertion,"[23] but he was unable to represent the health of the operatives who had been through it as in any way worse than that of most other classes of the community, even of the more wealthy classes. He was hardly less indignant over the schools which the children of the well-to-do were forced to attend than he was over factories. It is surprising that the relevance of his evidence has not been more widely realized. Hutchins and Harrison give one quotation from his book but entirely ignore his general conclusions.[24]

The contribution of Gaskell[25] (also a medical man) is valuable for the same reason as that of Thackrah,

22. *Effects of the Principal Arts*, etc., p. 222.

23. *Ibid.*, p. 45.

24. They refer to Dr. Turner Thackrah as "Dr. Thackrah Turner," an error which is repeated in the Index. Apparently they never noticed this mistake, for it persisted in the second edition of their *History*, published after an interval of eight years.

25. *Op. cit.*

namely, that he was an avowed antagonist of the factory system.[26] His work is well known, but it appears to have exercised so little influence on most discussions of this subject that some examination of his opinions seems desirable here.

He gave no support to the view that the coming of the factories had coincided with the economic degradation of the workers. On the contrary, he was quite clear that, apart from the effect on the hand-loom weavers, it had resulted in abundant material progress and that the wages of cotton operatives, "with proper economy and forethought, would enable them to live comfortably, nay, in comparative luxury."[27] It was the *moral* degradation of the worker that worried Gaskell. He condemned factories for the *vice* which he thought they had been instrumental in producing through causing the operatives to lose their "independence."[28] Children were forced to spend their

26. It was thought desirable in an argument amounting to a defense of the early factory system to quote chiefly from the evidence of opponents, but the most telling arguments in its favor are to be found in the writings of interested parties, Baines, Dr. Ure, and R. H. Greg. There is so voluminous a mass of material from the various commissions and committees that it would be possible to make out a case for almost any contention by a judicious selection of passages from them; but, read critically, they are enlightening.

27. *Op. cit.*, p. 216.

28. "Loss of independence" is a vague, much-used, and much-abused phrase. One of the main social results of the factory regime seems to have been the evolution of the idea of a wage *contract*, replacing the former idea of servitude. In the *Second Report of the Factory Commission* (1834) we notice the words "independence," or "inde-

most impressionable years amid surroundings of the utmost immorality and degradation, and he painted a truly appalling picture.

It seems to the writer a fact of the deepest significance that, in spite of Gaskell holding these opinions, and in spite of his regarding factory labor in general as "singularly unfitted for children," he could not bring himself to advocate the abolition of child labor. "The employment of children in manufactories," he wrote, "ought not to be looked upon as an evil, till the present moral and domestic habits of the population are completely re-organised. So long as home education is not found for them, and they are left to live as savages, they are to some extent better situated when engaged in light labour, and the labour generally is light which falls to their share."[29] It was the home life of children, prior to their factory days, which primarily led to such physical degeneracy as there was, and Gaskell emphasized this view. "This condition, it must be constantly borne in mind, has nothing to do with labour—as yet the child has undergone none."[30]

---

pendent," used over and over again, by employer witnesses living in all parts of the country (over five hundred put in evidence), as being the most obvious ones to use in describing the attitude of the operatives. The words were generally used in reply to a question about intimidation by the masters.

29. Gaskell, *op. cit.*, p. 209.

30. *Ibid.*, p. 198. It is interesting to note that Gaskell did not share the common belief that factory life stunted the intellectual faculties; he believed it had the reverse effect. He also denied the frequently

Can we decide how far the appalling immorality which Gaskell believed to exist in his day was due to the new industrial regime? He undoubtedly very much exaggerated the extent of the vice and degradation which existed. A Poor Law Commission some years before had painted a very gloomy picture, and he seems to have accepted quite uncritically the charges made by opponents of the system.[31] About 1830 a whole crop of literature bemoaning the morals of the people had burst forth, and it may, perhaps, be enlightening for us to examine an essay, dated 1831, which, although published anonymously, seems to have influenced and perhaps inspired many of the subsequent writers in a like vein.[32] It was entitled *An Enquiry into the State of the Manufacturing Population*. Not only was Gaskell influenced by it, but Dr. J. P. Kay's essay on *The Moral and Physical Condition of the Working Classes* (1832) was indebted to it, and a number of other contemporary works quoted from it. Hence we can fairly assume that the following compliment to a

---

made charge that the temperature and the composition of the atmosphere in which children worked was injurious to their health.

31. The commissioner, Tufnell, reported that "the whole current of testimony goes to prove that the charges made against cotton factories on the ground of immorality are calumnies" (Supplementary Report, D.2 [1834]).

32. The author was W. R. Greg, who, although a prolific essayist, never claimed this early effort, and it is indexed under *"Enquiry"* in the British Museum. He very soon reversed his opinions. See his article in the *Edinburgh Review*, 1849, p. 497.

foreign power expresses a point of view not uncommon in those days among the educated classes.

Spain, the most ignorant, degraded, and uncommercial of all countries pretending to civilisation is, in respect of crimes against property, *three times* less vicious than France, and *more than seven times less* vicious than England. This fact is a fearful one and speaks volumes. Spain ranks *cannibalism* among her list of crimes, but robbery is *rare, and petty theft still rarer.*

The factories were blamed for this. The weight that can be attached to such opinions can be judged by a further quotation from the same essay in which tea-drinking is condemned as a sign of demoralization!

"Under any circumstances we should deprecate the too liberal use of weak tea, as extremely debilitating to the stomach; but the practice is fatal to the constitution of all hard working men . . . it affords a temporary relief at the expense of a subsequent reaction, which, in its turn, calls for another and stronger stimulus." This led to the mixing of gin in the tea, a practice which prevailed "to an inconceivable extent among our manufacturing population." This is no attempt to ridicule by a carefully chosen passage from a crank. The opinion was common. Dr. J. P. Kay (who later became famous as Sir James Kay-Shuttleworth) said exactly the same thing in almost the same words the following year.[33]

33. J. P. Kay, *The Moral and Physical Condition of the Working Classes* (London, 1832).

It is but one case of the kind of argument which we constantly find, intended to prove that moral degradation had resulted from the factories and illustrated by examples which could quite easily suggest to us economic *and* social advance. Thackrah lamented the fact that children were no longer contented with "plain food" but must have "dainties."[34] The Reverend G. S. Bull deplored the tendency of girls to buy pretty clothes "ready-made" from shops instead of making them themselves, as this practice unfitted them to become "the mothers of children."[35] Gaskell saw decadence in tobacco. "Hundreds of men may be daily seen inhaling the fumes of this extraordinary plant."[36] He also saw moral decline in the growth of workmen's combinations. The men were no longer "respectful and attentive" to their "superiors."[37]

The factory owners' most usual reply to the charge of immorality against the factory operatives was to the effect that, in so far as there was any truth in such a charge, the cause could be found in irreligion. But this way of thinking was general in all camps. Gaskell lamented the frequent absence of a belief "of a state of future rewards and punishments. . . . Thus deprived of the most en-

---

34. Thackrah's evidence before Sadler's Committee, *op. cit.*, p. 514.

35. Sadler's *Report*, p. 423.

36. Gaskell, *op. cit.*, p. 110.

37. Gaskell, *Artisans and Machinery* (London, 1836), p. 22.

nobling characteristic of the human mind, what wonder can be felt that it is a wild waste?"[38]

Of the specific causes suggested for such decadence as there appeared to be, there are two which seem to have *some* plausibility. The first is the high earnings of the operatives which led to intemperance. Both Thackrah and Gaskell treat this as axiomatic. "The pocket-book makers have high wages and are not compelled to keep hours. Hence they are often very dissipated."[39] "The high wages allowed in some departments, induce drunkenness and improvidence."[40] "Higher wages, moreover, very often, if not generally, lead men to intemperance."[41]

The second suggestion, which seems to have some measure of truth, is that moral degradation was due to the flood of Irish immigrants who came over to take the place of those children who were forced out of industry by the Factory Acts. The children's wages, seldom more than from four to five shillings a week, were, neverthe-less, a big inducement to a race as poor as the Irish. Engels believed that the continued expansion of English industry could never have occurred had there not been this reserve at hand.[42] They were described as "an un-civilised race," and it may be that their inferior social tradition reacted upon the rest of the population. As they

38. Gaskell, *Manufacturing Population*, pp. 282–83.

39. Thackrah, *op. cit.*, p. 24.   40. *Ibid.*, p. 111.

41. Thackrah, before Sadler's Committee.

42. Engels, *op. cit.*, p. 90.

replaced children, the effect upon wages was probably not very great. Family earnings must have suffered, particularly where the displaced children could not get work in the mines or agriculture. Dobb's suggestion that the influx of Irish had the effect of depressing wages "to a brutally low level"[43] is certainly not borne out by the available statistics.[44]

The most impressive of the condemnations of the early factory system is the charge that it produced deformities and stunted growth in children. It is said that Oastler had noticed for many years the prevalence of deformity and lameness among factory operatives but that the causes were unknown to him. One day a friend informed him "to his horror" that these deformities were due to their lives in factories. He was "deeply impressed with all he had heard," and the very next morning he sat down and wrote his celebrated letter to the *Leeds Mercury* on "Yorkshire Slavery."[45] But we find that there was a general and widespread prevalence of deformities at that time,[46] and they seemed to be quite independent of the occupation pursued. There is ample confirmation of this

43. M. H. Dobb, *Capitalist Enterprise and Socialist Progress* (London, 1925), p. 331.

44. Bowley, *Wages in the United Kingdom* (Cambridge: Cambridge University Press, 1900), table facing p. 119.

45. Samuel Kydd, *History of the Factory Movement* (London, 1857), I, 96–98.

46. Andrew Combe, *Principles of Physiology* (2d ed.; London, 1834). Combe blamed the practice of swaddling and bandaging infants more than anything else for the presence of deformities (p. 159).

opinion in the evidence from many sources contained in the reports issued by the Factory Commission in 1833 and 1834.[47] That the contrary impression gained credence seems to have been entirely due to the energetic propaganda of Ashley, Oastler, Sadler, and their supporters. If there *was* a slightly larger proportion of deformity or puniness among the factory children, this might be accounted for by bearing in mind the frequent statement that children who were insufficiently strong for other employments were sent to the cotton factories because of the lightness of the work there.[48]

William Cooke Taylor tells of a cripple, deformed from birth, who was "exhibited as a kind of show in the hall of a benevolent nobleman," a spectacle that was repeated night after night to impress upon the fashionable world of London the belief that this unhappy wretch was a fair specimen of the injurious results produced by factory labor.[49] He was also paid to go on tour for this purpose. Later, he offered his services to the manufacturers, to expose the methods of the party that had origi-

47. One of the commissioners (Cowell), to test the charge that factory children were stunted, took the trouble *to ascertain their ages* and then measure and weigh them. Their average height was found to be identical with that of nonfactory children. Their average weight was slightly less. Cowell attributed this to the relative lightness of their work.

48. See evidence before the Lord's Committee, Sessional Papers, 1818, Vol. IX.

49. William Cooke Taylor, *The Factory System* (London, 1844), pp. 71 and 72.

nally engaged him, an offer which was "unfortunately refused."[50]

The propagandists had an excellent social medium in which to carry on their work. There never was an age more fond of sickly sentiment. It was the age of Mrs. Hemans, and is it to be wondered at that many of her admirers sought inspiration for tears in the factories? Mrs. Trollope and Mrs. Browning (Elizabeth Barrett) found in them a useful theme, and even Sadler was prompted to perpetrate "The Factory Child's Last Day" in the approved style.

It was easy to make an impression on the Tories, who for the most part not only were ignorant of the conditions in the factories[51] but were predisposed to condemn the factory owners. "The ancient feeling of contempt," says Ure, "entertained by the country gentlemen towards the burghers . . . is still fostered by the panegyrists of their order, and displayed itself, not equivocally, in the late Parliamentary crusade against the factories."[52] The chil-

50. Robert Blincoe, whose *Memoirs* had so strong an influence, may have lent his name to a more or less true story; but, in spite of his supposed sufferings, he lived to old age and was described by Samuel Kydd as being, in 1857, "a comparatively prosperous man."

51. Even Lord Shaftesbury "declined an offer to guide him through the principal spinning establishments as gratuitous and unnecessary" (William Cooke Taylor, *op. cit.*, p. 11), and Sir Robert Peel, a factory owner, was, according to Andrew Ure, but little conversant with the nature and condition of the cotton trade (*Philosophy of Manufactures* [3d ed.; London, 1861], p. 6).

52. Ure, *op. cit.*, p. 277.

dren were thought of as slaves, and the advantage of the considerable wages which they brought to their families was not put into the balance; neither was there any attempt to compare them to the poor of other sections of the community. This attitude goaded William Cooke Taylor into the deepest irony. People entered, or imagined that they entered, a mill and saw the little factory hands engaged in monotonous routine; and they thought "how much more delightful would have been the gambol of the free limbs on the hillside; the sight of the green mead with its spangles of buttercups and daisies; the song of the bird and the humming of the bee . . . [but] we have seen children perishing from sheer hunger in the mud hovel, or in the ditch by the wayside."[53] Compared to the factory workers, the agricultural laborers lived in abject poverty, and the work to which country children were put was far more exhausting than factory labor.[54] It was, however, "rarely witnessed by casual spectators except during fine weather."[55] Lord Shaftesbury, asked by Thorold Rogers why he had not sought to extend protective legislation to children in the fields when he knew that their work "was to the full as physically injurious" as premature labor in the factories, replied that it was a question of practical politics, and that, if he had

53. William Cooke Taylor, *op. cit.*, pp. 23 and 24.

54. Weeding, stone-picking, potato-planting, etc.

55. William Cooke Taylor, *op. cit.*, p. 26.

sought the emancipation of all, he would have obtained the support of no party at all.[56]

The millowners were, if anything, apathetic toward the antifactory propaganda. William Cooke Taylor says that they were persuaded that the calumnies which were circulated would never have been credited, but that their silence in trusting to the common sense of their countrymen was taken for a confession of guilt.[57]

Some of the exaggerations die hard.[58] For instance, the Hammonds twice repeat Fielden's statement that he had found from actual experiment that the factory child walked twenty miles a day in the course of his work in the mill.[59] Fielden never explained this experiment. He said that he would not "go into minute details" of his calculation because he would be "obliged to use terms that the ordinary reader would not understand."[60] Pos-

56. Thorold Rogers, *The Economic Interpretation of History* (London, 1888), p. 355.

57. *Op. cit.,* p. 11.

58. The growth of a vested interest in a class of state-employed factory inspectors seems to have helped to keep in the limelight the supposed horrors of unregulated industry. A comparison of the writings of Whately Cooke Taylor (a factory inspector) with those of his father, William Cooke Taylor, certainly suggests this. Compare Herbert Spencer's prophetic remarks on the "pressing desire for careers," in upper- and middle-class families and its encouragement to legislative control (*The Man versus the State* [R.P.A. ed.; London, 1884], p. 28).

59. *The Town Labourer,* p. 158, and *Lord Shaftesbury,* p. 44. This charge could only apply to those children engaged upon a particular process, "piecing." The Hammonds do not trouble to make this clear.

60. *Op. cit.*

sibly he thought his estimate moderate, as Condy tried to show that altogether they walked about thirty miles in a day! As a matter of fact R. H. Greg *did* make detailed calculations and set them forth clearly. The average distance a piecer could cover in a day he showed to be not more than eight miles.[61]

Let us try to take a balanced and detached view of conditions in those days, at the same time passing judgments only in the light of contemporary standards. The salient fact, and one which most writers fail to stress, is that, in so far as the work people then had a "choice of alternative benefits," they chose the conditions which the reformers condemned. Not only did higher wages cause them to prefer factory work to other occupations, but, as some of the reformers admitted, when one factory reduced its hours, it would tend to lose its operatives as they would transfer their services to establishments where they could earn more. The support of the artisan class for the Factory Acts could be obtained only by persuading them that as a result they would get the same or more money for less work. It was believed that technical considerations made it impossible for children's hours to be reduced without a corresponding reduction being conceded to adults, and the "Ten Hours' Movement" (as Hutchins and Harrison do not deny) was only concerned in its public utterances with the welfare of the children. Later, the operatives were brought to look upon children

61. R. H. Greg, *op. cit.*

as competitors to themselves, and this possibly acted as an even stronger motive in the support of the Factory Acts, particularly when the idea of working children in shifts developed.

We can ignore the platitude that the child, at least, was not a free agent. There were two lines of argument. On one side, "Against none do children more need protection than against their own parents"; and, on the other, "The parent is the only natural and efficient guardian of the child." We shall not attempt to value the implications involved in these ideas, but the second one is significant. The human emotions from which parental affections spring were no different then from what they are today, and it is to the different social and economic medium in which they were expressed that we must look for the cause of apparent callousness and cruelty.

It is hard to believe that rich philanthropists felt more strongly than parents about the welfare of their children. Protection against the effects of drunkenness may, perhaps, have been needed, but, in general, upper-class support for legal restrictions on child labor was based upon a complete lack of understanding of the difficulties with which the working masses had to contend.

Until the development of the industrial system had caused a general rise in material prosperity, such restrictions could only have added misery. No careful attempt to estimate the sufferings of children who were driven from employment by the various Factory Acts is known to the writer. Their condition was described by some of the first factory inspectors appointed in 1833, but the evil was soon lost sight of in the general prosperity following.[62]

There would have been *some* fall in hours and some elimination of child labor following increasing real wages, legislation or no legislation.[63] Both are expressions of a demand for leisure, and leisure is only demanded after the more primary of human wants are amply satisfied.

Moreover, until man has something to do in leisure, or until the commodities for use in leisure are sufficiently cheap and plentiful, what is the use of it to him? When he has these things, he can make a "choice between benefits," between leisure and other things. Legal enactments often enforce the choice of an authority, which thinks it knows better. Perhaps, in the case of factory legislation, the authority was, indirectly, right. By bringing the operative a greater degree of leisure "artificially," it may have taught him to value it for its own sake and

62. Gaskell admitted a short time after the Factories Regulation Act had been passed that, in causing large numbers of children to be turned adrift, it had only "increased the evils it was intended to remedy, and must, of necessity be repealed" (*Artisans and Machinery*, p. 67).

63. The elimination of child labor was, in part, due to technical changes. The development of steam power led to the use of larger machines less suitable for children to work with. Strangely enough, among the banners carried in the processions of the "Ten Hours' Movement," we find not only "No Child-Murder" but "Muzzle the Monster Steam" (Kydd, *op. cit.*, p. 61).

prefer it to the extra money which he habitually spent in the "alehouse" or the "dram shop." But until the Industrial Revolution had so far advanced as to bring other and more desirable things into competition with those institutions, it is possible that reduced hours may have had the reverse effect and led him to waste even more of his income than formerly. In the same way the moral welfare of children was probably safer in the factory than in the home before the social and moral changes, which the new industrial system made possible, had matured.

That the apparent benefits wrought by the early Factory Acts are largely illusory is suggested by the steady improvement which was undoubtedly taking place before 1833, partly as a result of the development of the factory system itself. All authorities, it is believed, admit that conditions were at their worst where domestic work prevailed and in the smaller factories and workshops, and there was a constant tendency for these to be eliminated through the competition of larger and more up-to-date establishments. The effect of the Act of 1833 was actually to set up a countertendency, for work was inclined to drift to workshops and the smaller factories which were more easily able to evade its provisions.

The chief obstacle to amelioration appears to have been apathy—the apathy of ignorance—rather than the cupidity of manufacturers. Masters and men, particularly the men, simply could not be brought to believe that certain practices were dangerous or injurious to health. The

operatives were very slow to learn. Efforts to improve the
factories had to be carried out in face of the opposition
of the very workers whom it was intended to benefit.
One millowner was threatened with a strike because he
installed a ventilating machine, and the spinners said
that it increased their appetites; the substitution of zinc
paint for white lead to prevent "painters' colic" was opposed by the painters; and the Sheffield grinders for
years fought against the introduction of the magnetic
mouthpiece. But it was not until the sixties and seventies,
when the ignorance of the operatives had been largely
overcome, that "dangerous trades," as such, were sub-
jected to state regulation.

The effect of the Factory Acts upon production is a
question which has not been squarely faced in modern
treatises. There was obviously a sacrifice of productive
power.[64] This sacrifice can, no doubt, be shown to have
been good, for social reasons, but the economic loss cannot be overlooked. In the case of children's labor the
effects went further than the mere loss of their work;
they lost their training and, consequently, their skill as
adults. A child can acquire dexterity much more easily

64. "Obviously" may seem an exaggeration in view of many vague
arguments to the reverse effect. The most confident of the writers who
put the cart before the horse was George Gunton, who argued that
"the standard of living and, consequently, the total income of the
family, is the lowest where the wife and children contribute the most
towards its support" (*Wealth and Progress* [London, 1888], p. 171).

than an adult, but such skill acquired in childhood is not easily lost.

Some critics seem to imagine that, when they have exploded Senior's "last-hour theory," they have proved that no reduction of output followed shorter hours. We get vague theories about "the economy of short hours." Shorter hours were not obtained without sacrifice; they may be said to have been purchased by the workers in their acceptance of diminished wages and by the community in lower productivity. The fact that these results are not easily discernible arises entirely from the general increase of wealth which continued through the century and which made possible and itself caused the demand for the leisure which the artisan class eventually possessed. Hutchins and Harrison make the common assumption that the reductions of hours were actually a main cause of the greater productivity which followed. They do not realize, apparently, that this is inconsistent with their argument that manufacturers were prevented from reducing hours of their own accord, because the force of competition gave an unfair advantage to those who did not make reductions. How far there is any truth in the theory of the economy of short hours will depend entirely upon the particular process concerned; in some cases output will be reduced proportionately, in others, less than proportionately, with curtailments of the working day.

The two main conclusions suggested by this discussion

are, first, that there has been a general tendency to exaggerate the "evils" which characterized the factory system before the abandonment of laissez faire and, second, that factory legislation was not essential to the *ultimate* disappearance of those "evils." Conditions which modern standards would condemn were then common to the community as a whole, and legislation not only brought with it other disadvantages, not readily apparent in the complex changes of the time, but also served to obscure and hamper more natural and desirable remedies.